AN
EASY
DICTIONARY

Compiled by
W. L. DARLEY

SCHOFIELD & SIMS LTD.
HUDDERSFIELD

First Edition February, 1961

Reprinted four times 1961

Sixth impression January, 1962

Seventh impression November, 1962

Eighth impression December, 1963

Ninth impression October, 1964

Tenth impression July, 1965

Eleventh impression August, 1966

Twelfth impression June, 1967

Thirteenth impression May, 1968

Fourteenth impression April, 1969

Revised and Reprinted 1970

PRINTED IN ENGLAND BY
WILLMER BROTHERS LTD
BIRKENHEAD
BOUND IN SCOTLAND

FOREWORD

"Junior school children should be able to use a dictionary and should have one in their desk for reference."—*Primary Education, Her Majesty's Stationery Office*, 1959.

Modern teaching methods demand that children should have access to reference books of all descriptions and should know how to use them. A dictionary is the first and probably the most important reference book that the child will need.

The aim in producing this dictionary has been to bridge the gap between the picture dictionary of the Infant (First) school and the formal dictionaries prepared for the use of older children. The book is intended primarily for the child of seven to nine years, though it will be found that its use will not be limited to this particular age group.

The dictionary contains almost 5,000 words, including derivatives, most of which are used in sentences which will help the child to understand the meaning of the word. Approximately 200 of the vocabulary words are also used in sentences.

In framing the definitions, simplicity has been combined with accuracy. When a word has more than one meaning, the different meanings have been arranged and numbered in order (e.g. the word 'account'). Where two words are spelt alike but are pronounced differently, the words are defined individually and their pronunciation is indicated by underlining the accented syllable (see 'record' and 'record').

It may be found that in some definitions, a word is given that is more difficult than the vocabulary word. For this early age group it is impossible, in all instances, to give a meaning that is simpler than the vocabulary word and at the same time to define the word accurately. The word 'car', for instance, is defined as 'a motor vehicle to carry people'. It can be argued that the word 'vehicle' is more difficult to understand than the word 'car'. It should be remembered, however, that:—

1. The child's vocabulary is thus being extended by the use of the dictionary.

2. The word 'vehicle' is clearly defined in the dictionary.

The definitions in some cases will be found to be more lengthy than those usually encountered in more adult dictionaries. This has been done so that a really clear explanation may be given within the vocabulary of the child.

Words which can be used both as nouns and as verbs are usually defined in one way only, dependent upon common usage.

In selecting the content, care has been taken to include words most needed by the child. It is inevitable, however, that words will be omitted which, in the opinion of some, should have been included, and for this, the compiler can only claim that it is impossible to include in a dictionary for pupils of this age range, all the words that might be required by the bright pupils. Again, it is emphasised that the dictionary is to bridge the gap between the picture dictionary (with its very limited vocabulary) and the more formal dictionaries.

"Children should be encouraged to make use of the standard dictionaries, which should be available, in addition to individual dictionaries, in each classroom". . . . *Primary Education, H.M.S.O.* 1959.

The appendix to the dictionary has been devised to be of value to the children in their written work and will be consulted frequently by them when they realise its scope.

The usefulness of the Companion book of Exercises, *Look It Up*, cannot be overemphasised. The exercises have been compiled on the assumption that the child has never before handled a dictionary and has no conception of alphabetical arrangement. Each exercise is designed to take the child a little further in his use of the dictionary, so that by the time a child has worked through the thirty exercises, he will be able to use a dictionary, or any similar book of reference, usefully and intelligently.

The book is presented in the hope that it will fill a need in a most important part of the school and that it will prove to be of real value to the children for whom it is intended.

I must take this opportunity to thank those people without whose help, advice and encouragement this book would not have been possible.

W.L.D.

AN EASY DICTIONARY

WITH APPENDIX
Pages 134—143

abandon	to leave. The sailors **abandoned** the sinking ship.
abbess	the head nun in a nunnery.
abbey	a church: a place where monks may live.
abbot	the head monk in an abbey.
abbreviation	a shortened word. Mr. (Mister): Rd. (Road).
abide	to dwell: to stay.
ability	being able to do things.
ablaze	on fire.
able	clever. 'John **is able to** swim' means: 'John **can** swim.'
aboard	on a ship.
abode	a house: a place to live.
abolish	to destroy.
abound	to have very many. Fish **abound** in the sea.
about	nearly: concerning.
above	over: higher than.
abreast	one beside the other. We walk into school two **abreast.**
abroad	a long way away: in another country.
abrupt	very quick: sudden. The story ended **abruptly.**
abscess	a painful boil.
absent	not here: not present. John's **absence** from school was caused by illness.
absolutely	quite: completely. I am **absolutely** sure.
absurd	foolish: stupid: silly.
abundance	plenty: a supply that is more than enough.
abundant	plentiful.
accent	the way we speak. He spoke with a foreign **accent.**
accept	to receive something which is offered or given.
accident	something unpleasant that happens without warning.
accompany	to go with.
accomplish	to finish doing something.
account	1. a story. 2. to explain how something happened. 3. a bill showing money to be paid.
accurate	exactly right.
accuse	to blame somebody.
ache	a pain in a part of the body: tooth**ache**: ear**ache**: head**ache.**
acorn	the seed of the oak tree.
acquaintance	a person who is known to us.
acrobat	a clever jumper. The **acrobat** performed at the circus.
across	from one side to the other: **across** the river.
act	1. something we do. 2. a part of a play. 3. to perform on the stage.
action	what we do when we act or move.
active	always moving about.
actor	a man who performs in a play or film.

actress	a woman who performs in a play or film.
add	to count: to total. He did an **addition** sum.
adder	a small poisonous snake.
address	1. the place where we live. 2. the place to which a letter is sent. 3. to write to: to speak to.
adjective	a word which describes.
adjoin	near together. He lived at the **adjoining** house.
admirable	excellent: very good indeed.
admiral	an officer of high rank in the Navy.
admire	to like very much.
admit	1. to agree that something has happened. 2. to allow somebody or something to enter.
adopt	to take a child and care for it.
adore	to worship: to love dearly.
adrift	floating on water helplessly in a boat or on a raft.
advance	to move forward.
adventure	an exciting happening.
advertise	to make well-known.
advice	what we say to people when we advise them.
advise	to tell other people what we think they should do.
aerial	a wire which sends out or picks up wireless or television signals.
aerodrome	an airfield where aeroplanes arrive and depart.

aeroplane	a flying machine.
afar	far away.
affect	to cause things to change.
affection	love for something or somebody.
afford	to be able to pay for.
afloat	floating.
afraid	full of fear: frightened.
after	behind: following.
afternoon	between mid-day and evening.
again	once more.
against	1. opposite to: on the opposite side. The two teams played **against** each other. 2. upon: beside. The spade was placed **against** the tree.
age	1. how old a person is. 2. a special time in history such as the **Stone Age.**
aggravate	1. to make somebody angry. 2. to make things worse.
aglow	shining.
ago	in the past: a long time **ago.**
agony	great pain.
agree	to think the same as.
agreeable	1. pleasant and friendly. 2. willing.
aground	held in sand or rocks in shallow water.
ahead	in front of: before.
aid	to give help to another.

aim	1. to point at a target. 2. to attempt to do something.
air	1. what we breathe. 2. to warm. Mother **airs** clothes. 3. a tune. She sang an **air.**
airport	a place where passengers land and from where they depart in air liners.
ajar	partly open. The door was **ajar.**
alarm	1. a warning. 2. a sudden fright.
alas	what a pity. We hoped for sunshine, but ,**alas,** it rained.
album	a collection of things such as stamps in a book.
alert	always ready to act.
alight	1. on fire. 2. to step down from.
alive	living.
all	everything: everyone.
alley	a narrow passage.
alligator	a kind of crocodile.
allotment	land used for a garden.
allow	to permit: to let us do something.
ally	a friend who helps us to do something.
almond	1. a nut used in cooking. 2. the tree on which the nut grows.
almost	nearly: not quite. We were **almost** there.
alms	gifts to poor people.

aloft	high up: above.
alone	by oneself: with nobody else there.
along	from one end to the other.
aloud	with a loud voice.
alphabet	the A B C.
already	now: at present: beforehand.
also	as well.
altar	the holy table in church.
alter	to change. The boy made an **alteration** in his book.
although	though: even if.
altogether	counting everybody. **Altogether** there are six of us.
always	for ever.
amaze	to surprise: to astonish. The story filled us with **amazement.**
amble	to walk slowly.
ambulance	a van to carry sick or injured people: a hospital bus.
amen	the ending of a prayer.
amid	in the middle of.
amiss	wrong: not working properly.
among amongst	in the middle of: with others all round.
amount	1. a sum of money. 2. a number: a quantity.
ample	quite enough: sufficient.
amuse	to please: to make us laugh.
ancestor	a forefather.

anchor	a heavy metal hook to stop a ship from moving.
ancient	very old: belonging to times of long ago.
angel	one who brings messages from God.
anger	rage: when we are not pleased. The children were **angry** with the boy who spoilt the game.
angle	a corner.
angler	a man who fishes with rod and line.
animal	a living creature.
ankle	the joint between the leg and the foot.
announce	to make known by telling.
announcer	one who makes things known.
annoy	to make angry: to tease.
annoyance	something that annoys us.
annual	1. happening every year. 2. a book which comes out each year.
anoint	to pour oil over a person's head on a special occasion such as when a king is crowned.
anorak	a short coat.
another	one more.
answer	1. what we are asked to find out or to work out. 2. to reply.
antelope	a sort of deer which is found in Africa.
anvil	a metal block on which hot metal is hammered.
anxious	worried.

any	one of many: some.
apart	separate: aside.
apartments	lodgings: rooms in a house for which we pay.
ape	a large monkey.
apostle	a preacher: a follower.
appeal	to ask for: to beg for.
appear	to show oneself: to become visible. The clown's **appearance** caused us to laugh.
appendix	pages added at the end of a book.
appetite	the wish to eat.
apple	the fruit of the apple tree.
appoint	to give a job to.
approach	to come near to.
approve	to be pleased with something.
apricot	a fruit which we eat and which is rather like a plum.
apron	a piece of cloth worn to keep our clothes clean.
aquarium	a tank or bowl for fish.
arch	a curved part of a building or bridge.
area	the space covered, often by a piece of land or water. The flood covered a large **area.**
argue	not to agree with somebody. There was an **argument** when they met.
arise	to rise from: to get up.
arithmetic	working in numbers.
ark	the boat built by Noah before the flood.

arm	the part of the body between the shoulder and the hand.
armour	metal clothes worn by knights in battle.
army	a large number of soldiers.
around	round the edges of: on all sides.
arouse	to wake from sleep.
arrange	1. to put in the right order. 2. to make plans. The **arrangements** for the party had been made.
arrive	to reach the place to which we are going. The train whistle told of its **arrival.**
arrow	the straight sharp piece of wood which is shot from a bow.
article	1. a thing. 2. a piece of writing in a newspaper.
artificial	not natural: made by man.
artist	a person who is clever at drawing, craftwork or music.
ascend	to go upwards: to climb up.
ash	1. the remains of a fire. 2. the name of a tree.
ashamed	to be very sorry about something.
ashore	on the shore: on land.
aside	to one side.
ask	1. to demand. 2. to beg.
asleep	sleeping.
aspirin	a medicine taken to lessen such pains as headache.
assembly	a group of people.
assist	to give help to. The lady asked for our **assistance.**
astern	at the back of a boat
astonish	to surprise. We were filled with **astonishment** at what had happened.
astray	wandering away.
astronaut	a space man.
atmosphere	air round the earth.
attack	to start to fight: to set upon.
attempt	to try to do something.
attend	1. to be present. An **attendance** register. 2. to listen to. 3. to look after.
attention	1. care given to doing a job. 2. a position in which we stand perfectly upright.
attic	a room at the top of a house.
attire	dress: the clothes we wear.
attract	1. to win the liking of. 2. to make things come closer. The flowers were very **attractive.** The circus proved a great **attraction.**
audience	people who listen or watch.
aunt	father's or mother's sister: **auntie : aunty.**
author	a person who writes a book.
autumn	the season between summer and winter.
avalanche	when snow falls in great quantities down the sides of a mountain.
avenue	a road having trees along its sides.

avoid	to miss: to dodge.
await	to wait for.
awake	not asleep: wakened up. We tried not to **awaken** the baby.
award	to give a prize.
aware	knowing about something.
away	not here: not present.
awful	terrible: fearful.
awkward	clumsy.
axe	a kind of chopper or hatchet.
axle	the bar to which the wheels of a car or cart are fastened and on which they turn.

B

babe **baby** }	a young child: an infant.
bachelor	a man who is not married.
back	1. the rear part of anything. 2. to **come back** means to **return.**
backward	1. not clever: slow. 2. towards the back.
bacon	the flesh of the pig made ready to eat by salting.
bad	1. not good: evil. 2. rotten.
badge	a special sign pinned or stitched to the clothes to show that we belong to a school or team.
badger	a grey-haired animal which burrows in the ground.
badly	1. seriously: **badly** hurt. 2. greatly. I need it **badly.**
baffle	to puzzle.

bag	a container which has an open top.
baggage	1. luggage. 2. the trunks and cases in which we carry our clothes when travelling.
bail	1. the cross piece on the stumps at cricket. 2. to ladle water from the bottom of a boat. (See 'bale').
bailiff	a man in charge of land, water or property.
bait	something used in a trap or on a hook to attract an animal or a fish.
bake	to cook in an oven. The man carried the loaves from the **bakery.**
balance	1. to remain steady. 2. weighing scales.
balcony	1. a raised floor in a theatre or cinema. 2. a platform outside a window.
bald	having no hair on the head.
bale	1. a large parcel fastened with ropes or straps. 2. to ladle water from the bottom of a boat. (See 'bail').
ball	1. something round. 2. a large dancing party.
ballet	a graceful dance.
balloon	1. a round bag which rises into the air when filled with a gas which is lighter than air. 2. a toy of thin rubber which can be blown up.

bamboo	a grass with stiff, hollow stems used as canes in gardens.
banana	a yellow fruit shaped like a cigar.
band	1. a group of musicians playing together. 2. material used to hold things together or as a decoration. 3. a group of people.
bandage	a dressing used to cover a wound.
bandit	a thief, robber or highwayman.
bangle	a bracelet.
banish	1. to send away for a long time. 2. to send out of the country.
banister	a hand-rail beside a staircase.
banjo	a musical instrument which is played by plucking the strings.
bank	1. the side of a river. 2. a place where money may be kept for safety. 3. a pile of earth or sand with sloping sides. 4. to turn an aeroplane.
banknotes	paper money such as pound notes.
banner	a flag hanging from a pole, mast or rope.
banquet	a feast: a grand meal.
baptise	to dip into water as a sign that our sin is washed away.
bar	1. a rod of metal or of wood. 2. a division in music.
barber	a man who cuts men's hair.
bare	with nothing on: naked.
barely	hardly.
bargain	a useful thing bought cheaply.
barge	a boat which usually has a flat bottom and which is used on a canal or river.
bark	1. the noise made by a dog. 2. the covering round the wood of a tree.
barley	corn used in making beer.
barn	a store-house on a farm.
baron	a lord: a nobleman.
barrel	1. a round box. 2. the part of a gun through which the bullet is fired.
barren	not bearing fruit.
barrier	a fence or wall to hinder or stop.
barrow	a small hand-cart often with one wheel.
base	the bottom part: the lowest part.
basement	a room below the ground: a cellar.
basin	a dish or bowl.
basket	a bag or container made of cane.
bat	1. the wood used to strike the ball in cricket. 2. an animal which is like a mouse but which flies at night.
batch	a number of things together.
bath	a large tank in which we can wash or swim.
bathe	to swim or play in water.

battle	a fight between two groups of people.
bay	1. a place where the shore curves inwards. 2. a square or rounded window.
bazaar	1. a market in eastern lands. 2. a sale of goods to help a church or chapel.
beach	sand or pebbles at the sea shore.
beads	small round pieces of glass which are threaded on to a string.
beak	the mouth of a bird.
beaker	a cup without a handle.
beam	1. a large log of wood or metal. 2. a ray of light.
bean	a vegetable that we eat. Jack climbed the **beanstalk.**
bear	1. a wild animal, either black, brown or white. A **polar bear** is white. 2. to carry. It was too heavy for me to **bear.**
beard	hair growing on the face.
beast	1. an animal. 2. an unkind person.
beat	1. to smack with a cane or belt. 2. to keep time in music with a stick. 3. to win a game or battle. 4. to mix things by stirring them heavily and quickly.
beauty	prettiness: good looks: loveliness: a **beautiful** picture.
beaver	a small animal found in cold lands, near to water or in water.
because	for this reason. We could not go **because** it was raining.
beckon	to wave somebody to come.
become	to happen to: to come to be. I do not know what will **become** of you.
bed	the piece of furniture on which we sleep.
bee	an insect which collects honey from flowers. The queen **bee** was in the hive.
beech	a tree which has dark green leaves.
beef	the flesh or meat from cattle.
beer	a drink made from barley.
beet	a vegetable with a large root.
beetle	an insect with wings.
befall	to happen without it being expected.
before	1. in front of: earlier than. 2. in past times.
beggar	a person who asks for money or goods to be given to him.
begin	to start. The **beginning** of the story was most interesting.
behave	how we act in front of others. Our **behaviour** should be a credit to our school.

behind	at the back of.
behold	to look at: to see.
being	something that is alive.
belief	trust: what we feel to be true.
believe	to know that something is true: to trust in something.
bell	a piece of rounded metal which will ring when tapped.
bellows	an air pump to make a fire begin to blaze.
belong	1. to be our own. 2. to be a part of.
below	underneath: lower down.
belt	a narrow piece of material worn round the waist.
bench	1. a long wooden seat. 2. a table at which a man may work with tools.
bend	1. a turn: a curve. 2. to make something turned or curved.
beneath	under: below: in a lower place.
benefit	to do good to somebody.
beret	a small round hat.
berry	the juicy fruit of a plant.
berth	a bed on a ship, aeroplane or train.
beside	at the side of: next to.
betray	to tell about something when we have been trusted not to tell.
better	more good. I can do **better** than you. She had been ill, but now she was **better**.
between	1. in the middle of. 2. shared by several people.
beware	to be very careful of.
beyond	farther on than. The farm was **beyond** the end of the lane.
Bible	the Holy Scriptures.
bicycle	a two-wheeled machine that we can ride.
bier	a stretcher on which a coffin is carried.
bilberry	1. a small, blue, eatable fruit. 2. the bush on which the fruit grows.
bilious	when we have eaten something that makes us feel ill.
bill	1. a list that shows money that we owe. 2. The beak of a bird.
billiards	a ball game played on a table.
billows	huge waves on the sea.
bin	a large metal box.
bind	to wrap round with cord or string.
birch	a tree with a silvery bark.
bird	a feathered animal which has wings and can fly.
birthday	the day of the year when we were born.
biscuit	a thin baked food that we can eat.
bishop	the priest in charge of a large district such as a city.

bit	1. a small piece. 2. a piece of metal in a horse's reins held in the mouth. 3. a tool for making holes.
bite	to cut something with the teeth.
bitter	tasting sour: not good to taste.
black	the darkest colour: the opposite to white.
blackberry	a wild eatable fruit used in jam and tarts.
blacksmith	a man who uses tools to make things out of metal.
blade	1. the part of a knife or sword used for cutting. 2. the flat part of a leaf. 3. an oar. 4. the shoulder bone.
blame	to find fault with: to say who has done wrong.
blancmange	a sort of jelly which we eat.
blank	empty: with nothing written on it: perfectly plain.
blanket	a warm bed-covering made of wool.
blare	to make a loud disagreeable noise.
blast	1. a sudden rush of wind. 2. the sound made by bugles and trumpets. 3. the sound made by an explosion.
blaze	to burn with bright flames.
blazer	a light sports jacket often worn in warm weather.

bleach	to make something lighter or whiter in colour.
bleak	cold, windy and dismal.
bleat	the sound made by sheep and lambs.
bleed	what takes place when blood flows.
blend	to mix things together.
bless	1. to ask God to help somebody. 2. to wish happiness to.
blind	1. not to be able to see. 2. a screen for a window.
blink	to open and close the eyes quickly.
blister	a sore swelling on the skin.
blizzard	a strong wind with heavy snow.
block	1. a large piece of wood, stone or metal. 2. to be in the way of. 3. a line of buildings.
blond(e)	fair in colour.
blood	the red liquid in our veins.
bloom	a flower.
blossom	flowers of plants and trees.
blot	a dirty mark: an ink stain.
blotter	paper used to dry ink.
blouse	a light garment worn by girls and women on the top half of the body.
blow	1. to send out air from the mouth quickly. 2. when air moves fast. 3. a knock.
blue	the colour of the sky without clouds.
blunder	a stupid mistake.
blunt	not able to cut: not sharp.

blush	when our faces go red because we are ashamed or excited.
board	1. a flat piece of wood. 2. to go on a ship, train or aeroplane.
boast	to say how clever we are.
boat	a ship.
bobbin	a wooden reel to hold cotton.
body	1. a person. 2. the main part of anything. 3. a group of people.
bog	wet earth: a swamp. The ground beside the river was **boggy**.
boil	1. a swelling on the body. 2. when water is heated and turns into steam. 3. to cook in hot water.
bold	not afraid: brave.
bolster	a large pillow.
bolt	1. a fastener on a door. 2. a metal screw. 3. to fasten. 4. to rush away. 5. to gulp food.
bomb	a shell which explodes when it is dropped.
bone	the hard part of an animal's body.
bonfire	a large fire built in the open air for pleasure.
bonnet	1. a hat worn by women, children or babies. 2. the cover of a motor-car engine.
bonny	looking very healthy.

book	a number of pages fastened together.
boot	1. footwear which covers the ankles. 2. a covered place for luggage in a car.
border	1. the edge. 2. the place where neighbouring countries meet. We crossed the **border** between England and Scotland.
bore	1. to make a hole. 2. to talk to people without interesting them. We were **bored** because he spoke for so long.
born	when something or somebody becomes alive. Jesus Christ was **born** in Bethlehem.
borne	carried. The chest was **borne** by two men.
borrow	when somebody lends us something. I **borrowed** my brother's ball.
both	two things: two people together.
bother	1. trouble. Do not **bother** to come. 2. to annoy somebody. He promised not to **bother** us again.
bottle	a glass container fitted with a cork.
bottom	the underneath: the lowest part.
bough	the branch of a tree.
bought	paid for.

B

boulder   a large stone or rock.

bounce   to make something spring up and down.
We **bounced** the balls.

bound   1. forced to do something.
2. tied together.

boundary   1. the outside edge.
2. the line where one piece of land touches another.

bouquet   a very neat bunch of flowers. The bride carried a **bouquet.**

bow (like 'low') 1. ribbon with loops on it.
2. a weapon used to fire arrows.

bow (like 'now') 1. the front part of a boat.
2. to bend forward from the waist: to curtsy.
We **bowed** as the queen walked past.

bowl   1. a wide dish.
2. to send the ball to the batsman at cricket or rounders.

box   1. a wooden chest or case.
2. to fight with the fists.

boxer   a man who fights with his fists.

boy   a man child: a young male.

bracelet   a decoration worn on the wrist or arm.

brag   to boast: to think we are very clever.

braid   narrow material used to decorate the edges of clothing.

brain   the part of the head with which we think.

brake   the part on the vehicle which makes a vehicle go slower or stop.

bramble   a prickly bush on which blackberries grow.

branch   the part of the tree from which the leaves grow.

brand   to put a mark on something to show the owner or maker.
The farmer **branded** his sheep.

brass   a yellowish metal made from two other metals.

brave   1. not afraid.
2. an Indian warrior.

bravery   courage: valour.

bread   food made from baked flour, yeast and water.

break   1. to smash.
2. a short rest from what we are doing.

breakfast   the first meal of the day.

breath   the air we send out from our mouths and noses.

breathe   what we do when air passes in and out of our lungs.

breed   1. the family or race of an animal.
2. to have and bring up young ones.

breeze   a gentle wind.

brick   1. a baked clay block used for building.
2. square wooden blocks used by children as toys.

bride   the woman who is just married or is just going to be married.

bridegroom	the man who is just married or is just going to be married.	**brow**	1. the forehead. 2. the top of a hill.
bridge	1. something built by which we can cross over a stream, road or railway. 2. a platform for officers on a ship.	**brown**	a dark colour made by mixing red and yellow.
		bruise	a mark on the skin where it has been knocked.
brigade	a group of people such as soldiers, boys (Boys' Brigade), firemen (Fire Brigade).	**brush**	1. a tool used for sweeping, cleaning and scrubbing. 2. a fox's tail.
bright	1. brilliant: shining. 2. clever.	**bubble**	when water forms round gas or air.
brilliant	bright: shining: dazzling.	**bucket**	a container with a handle: a pail.
brim	1. the edge of a vessel such as a basin. 2. the part of a hat which sticks out at the edge.	**buckle**	1. a clasp on clothing. 2. to bend.
		bud	a leaf or flower before it opens.
bring	to carry with you.	**budge**	to move slightly.
brink	a dangerous edge like the edge of a cliff.	**bugle**	a musical wind instrument like a small trumpet.
brisk	lively: quick.	**build**	to put up: to erect. The new school was a fine **building.**
bristles	short and stiff hairs such as we find on a brush.		
brittle	hard yet easily broken.	**bulb**	1. a flower root which is shaped like an onion. 2. the part of an electric light that shines.
broad	very wide.		
brooch	an ornament which can be pinned to the clothing. The lady wore two **brooches.**		
		bulge	something that swells outwards.
brood	1. a number of young birds hatched together. 2. to think deeply and to worry when there is no need to do so.	**bull**	a male animal of cattle, elephant, whale and so on.
		bullet	a piece of metal shot from a gun or rifle.
brook	a tiny stream.	**bully**	someone who ill-treats those weaker than himself. The two **bullies** hurt the small boy.
broom	a stiff brush with a long handle.		
brother	a boy who has the same parents as ourselves.		

bump	a sudden knock.
bumper	a metal rail in front of and behind a vehicle.
bunch	several things of the same sort together. I bought a **bunch** of flowers.
bundle	many things fastened together.
bungalow	a house with all its rooms on one floor: a house with no 'upstairs'.
bunk	a bed fixed to a wall like a shelf: a bed on board a ship.
buoy	a floating object which is fastened and which warns ships of danger.
burden	a load: something that is carried.
burglar	a person who enters houses and shops to steal. The police were asking questions about the **burglary.**
burial	when somebody or something is buried.
burn	1. a sore place on the skin caused by heat. 2. to blaze.
burrow	an underground tunnel dug by an animal such as a rabbit.
burst	1. to blow into pieces: to explode. 2. to break open.
bury	to put under the ground.
bus	an omnibus: a motor-coach.
bush	a small tree: a shrub.

business	trade: work.
busy	having no time to spare.
butcher	a man who sells meat.
butler	the head man-servant over all the other servants.
butter	a fatty food made from milk.
butterfly	a flying insect grown from a caterpillar.
button	a small round fastening for clothing.
buy	to obtain something by giving money.
buzz	the sound made by some insects when flying.

C

cab	a carriage that we can hire: a taxi.
cabbage	a green vegetable that we can eat.
cabin	1. a room on a boat. 2. a small wooden house.
cabinet	a piece of furniture which has a glass front and which is sometimes fitted with drawers.
cable	1. several wires running side by side to carry electricity. 2. a strong rope often made of wires twisted together.
cackle	the noise made by hens or geese when they have laid an egg or when they are excited.
caddy	a small box to hold tea.
café	a place for eating: a restaurant.

cage	a box or room fitted with wires or bars and in which animals or birds are kept.
cake	a sweet food made from flour and baked in an oven.
calendar	a sheet or book showing the days and months of the year.
calf	a young animal, usually a young cow or bull. The **calves** were in the shed.
call	1. to shout to someone. 2. to visit someone. 3. to give a name to someone. He is **called** Tom.
caller	someone who calls.
calm	quiet and still: peaceful.
camel	an animal which has one or two humps and which is used for carrying goods and people in hot lands.
camera	a machine which takes photographs.
camp	1. a group of tents together. 2. to live in a tent. The scouts decided to **camp** near to the river.
can	1. a small container made of tin. 2. 'I **can** do it' means:— 'I **am able to** do it.'
canal	a river made by man for boats and barges to use.
canary	a yellow singing bird sometimes kept in houses.
cancel	1. to cross out. 2. to do away with.
candle	a piece of rounded wax with a wick which is burned to give light.
cane	1. a thin, round piece of wood. 2. the sugar plant.
cannibal	a man-eating savage.
cannon	a heavy gun which fires shells.
cannot	not able to do something.
canoe	a small, light boat moved by using a paddle.
cap	1. a head covering without a brim. 2. a lid or cover.
capable	able to do.
cape	a cloak to cover a person's shoulders and arms.
capital	1. the chief city or town. 2. a large letter such as A B Y or Z.
captain	the chief man of a group: the leader.
captive	a prisoner. The soldiers were taken into **captivity.**
capture	to take prisoner: to catch.
car	a motor vehicle to carry people.
caramel	a sweet made from brown sugar.
caravan	a house on wheels.
card	thick paper.
cardigan	a short woollen jacket.
care	1. using caution: attending to what we are doing. We must be **careful** when we cross roads. **Careless** work is often wrong. 2. to '**care for**' means:— to '**look after**'.

caretaker	a person who looks after a building such as a school.
cargo	goods carried on a ship.
carnival	a merry dance: a large party in special dress.
carol	a Christmas hymn.
carpenter	a man who makes the wooden parts of buildings and ships.
carpet	a large rug to cover a floor often made by weaving coarse material.
carriage	a cart or car for carrying people.
carrot	a reddish-brown, eatable, root vegetable.
carry	to take from one place to another. The porter **carried** the cases.
cart	a vehicle for carrying goods.
carton	a box made of cardboard.
carve	to shape wood or stone with cutting tools.
case	a box which has a lid and is often made of wood.
cash	money in notes and coins.
cashier	a person who looks after the money of a firm or shop.
cask	a barrel often used to store liquids.
casket	1. a small barrel. 2. a jewel box.
cast	1. to throw far away. 2. people taking part in a play.
castle	a stone building with towers and strong walls.

castor	a small wheel fitted to furniture so that it may be moved easily.
cat	a small furry animal often kept as a pet in a home.
catapult	an instrument for shooting stones.
catch	1. to take hold of. 2. a fastener for a door. 3. to trap. The butterfly was **caught** in a net.
caterpillar	the grub which will turn into a moth or butterfly.
cathedral	the most important church in a city: the church of a bishop.
catkin	the flower of the willow tree.
cattle	cows, oxen and bulls.
cauliflower	a vegetable with a white eatable flower.
cause	to make something happen.
causeway	a raised pavement.
caution	great care. We must cross roads with **caution.**
cave **cavern**	a hole in rocks or in the earth. We decided to explore the **cavern.**
caw	the noise made by rooks and crows.
cease	to stop doing something.
ceaseless	without stopping.
ceiling	the roof of a room.
celebrate	to remember something in a special way.
celery	a vegetable with long, white, eatable stalks.
cell	a room in which prisoners are kept.

cellar	a store room under a building.	**chance**	1. an unexpected happening. 2. a risk.
cement	a stone dust which sets hard when mixed with water.	**change**	1. money received back when we offer too much. 2. to alter. The weather was very **changeable.**
cemetery	a burial ground. The two **cemeteries** were side by side.	**channel**	a narrow strip of water.
cent	1. a coin of low value used in some countries. 2. a hundredth part.	**chapel**	a small church: a place of worship.
celsius	a temperature scale of 100 degrees formerly centigrade.	**chapter**	a part of a story or book.
centimetre **central**	a hundredth part of a metre. in the middle. The boy stood in the **central** place.	**character**	1. how we behave: our nature. 2. a person in a play or story.
centre	the middle of something.	**charge**	1. the money that is asked for when something is bought.
century	1. a hundred years. 2. a hundred runs at cricket. The two batsmen each scored **centuries.**		2. to rush at.
		chariot	a horse-drawn cart used in earlier times.
cereal	a corn crop used for food.	**charm**	1. a magic spell.
ceremony	a special service held to celebrate something.		2. to give pleasure to other people. She was a **charming** old lady.
certain	1. sure. It is **certain** that we shall go. I shall **certainly** come 2. some, but not all. **Certain** children went to the circus.	**chart**	1. a map used by sailors. 2. a drawing or a sketch.
		chase	to run after.
certificate	a paper proving that we can do, or have done, something.	**chasm**	a large hole in rock or in the ground.
		chat	to talk in a friendly way.
chain	a number of rings or links joined together.	**chatter**	to speak quickly and without thinking what we are saying.
chair	a seat which has a back rest and is for one person.		
chalk	1. a coloured crayon. 2. a white rock.	**chauffeur**	a man paid to drive a motor-car.
champion	the winner over all the others.	**cheap**	not expensive: low in price.

cheat	act unfairly: to deceive.
check	1. to make sure that everything is correct. 2. a pattern used on cloth. 3. to slow down.
cheek	1. the sides of the face between the nose and the ear. 2. rudeness.
cheer	1. to shout loudly for joy. 2. happiness. He was always **cheerful.**
cheese	a food made by beating milk or cream.
chemist	a man who sells medicines.
cherry	a small stony fruit.
chess	a game played by two people on a squared board.
chest	1. a large strong box. 2. the upper front part of the body.
chestnut	1. a tree that bears nuts. 2. a reddish-brown colour.
chick(en)	a young bird.
chief	the main one: the leader. The white men spoke with the Indian **chieftain.**
chiefly	mostly.
chilblains	itching on hands and feet caused by frosty weather.
child	a young boy or girl. The **children** were playing in the park.
chill	an illness caused by cold. In December, the days are often **chilly.**
chime	the noise made by bells.
chimney	a pipe to take smoke away.
chin	the part of the face below the bottom lip.
china	fine pottery such as thin cups and saucers.
chip	1. a tiny piece broken from a larger piece. 2. a piece of potato fried in fat.
chirp	the noise made by young birds.
chisel	a sharp steel tool used for cutting wood, stone or metal.
chocolate	a sweet food made from cocoa.
choir	a group of people singing together.
choke	1. to gasp for breath: to smother. 2. to block up.
choose	to pick out what is wanted from a large number. The girl was asked to make a **choice.**
chop	to cut with an axe.
christen	to baptise an infant and give it a name.
Christian	a believer in Jesus Christ.
Christmas	the time of the year when we remember the birth of Christ. **Christmas** Day:— 25th December.
chum	a close friend.
chunk	a thick piece cut off from something larger.
church	a building in which we worship God.

cigar	tobacco leaves rolled tightly together and used for smoking.
cigarette	tobacco leaves rolled into a paper tube for smoking.
cinder	a piece of coal which has been partly burned.
cinema	a place where films are shown.
circle	a round ring.
circular	1. something that is round in shape. 2. something that travels round. The man was using a **circular** saw.
circus	a travelling show of animals, actors and clowns.
cistern	a large tank to hold water.
city	a large town which often has a cathedral. The two **cities** were many miles apart.
civil	polite: showing good manners.
claim	to say that something belongs to us.
clang	the sound made by a large bell.
clap	1. the sound made by thunder. 2. to slap the hands together quickly.
clash	1. to bump together noisily. 2. to disagree with.
clasp	1. a fastening. 2. to grip or hold fast to something.
class	1. children who are taught together. 2. a group of people of the same sort.

clatter	a loud rattling noise.
claw	the hard nails of a bird or an animal.
clay	sticky earth from which bricks may be made.
clean	not dirty or dusty.
clear	easy to see. The clouds stood out **clearly.**
cleft	a crack: a split.
clergyman	a vicar: the man in charge of a church.
clerk	(say 'clark') a person who works in an office and who writes.
clever	able to do things easily: intelligent. The picture had been **cleverly** painted.
cliff	high steep land overlooking the sea.
climate	the sort of weather a place has.
climb	to walk up a steep place. The **climbers** were roped together.
cling	to hold tightly with the hands.
clinic	a place where doctors and nurses give help to people.
clip	1. a fastener. 2. to cut off, using scissors or shears.
cloak	a covering for the body and arms but having no sleeves.
clock	a machine for telling us the time.
clockwork	machinery which is worked by winding a spring. The toy engine was driven by a **clockwork** motor.

clog	to choke: to block up.
clogs	very heavy shoes made of wood, or with wooden soles.
close	(like 'dose') near. We sit **close** together.
close	(like 'doze') to shut. I forgot to **close** the door.
cloth	material to make clothes.
cloud	a mass of rainy mist in the sky. The sun was hidden on the **cloudy** day.
clover	a small flowering plant used to feed cattle.
clown	a man who acts foolishly to amuse people.
club	1. a heavy stick. 2. a group of people who meet together for a special purpose. 3. a stick used to play golf.
clue	a guide: something which helps in finding the answer to a puzzle or a question.
clumsy	awkward in the way we move.
cluster	a bunch or a group of things.
coach	a passenger vehicle such as a bus or a railway carriage.
coal	a black rock dug out of the ground and burned to make heat.
coarse	rough: not fine.
coast	where the sea and land meet: the seashore.
coat	1. an outer garment with sleeves. 2. the hair of an animal.

cobbler	a man who repairs boots and shoes.
cobweb	a net made by a spider to trap insects which it eats.
cock **cockerel**	a male bird.
cocoa	a brown powder from which we make chocolate.
coconut	the fruit of the coco palm tree.
cod	a large eatable sea fish.
code	writing with a hidden meaning.
coffee	a hot drink made from roasted and crushed seeds.
coffin	a box in which a dead body is carried.
coil	a band of wire or rope.
coin	a metal disc which is used as money.
coke	baked coal from which gas has been taken.
cold	1. not hot: chilly. 2. an illness.
collar	1. a neckband. 2. the part of our clothes which fits round the neck.
collect	to gather together. He had a large **collection** of stamps.
college	a place where students are taught.
collide	to crash: to bump together.
collision	a violent crash together.
colour	dye or paint.
column	1. a pillar of stone or wood. 2. a strip of printing in a book or newspaper. 3. a line of troops.

comb	an instrument with many teeth used for smoothing the hair.
combine	to join together: to unite.
come	to draw near to. We **came** to the house.
comfort	freedom from worry or trouble.
comfortable	cosy: contented.
comic	amusing: something that makes us laugh.
comma	a punctuation mark shaped ,
command	to order: to instruct.
commence	to begin: to start.
commit	to do something, usually something wrong.
common	ordinary and usual.
companion	a friend: a comrade.
compare	to see if things are alike.
compel	to force.
competition	a contest to find the best.
complain	to grumble: to find fault.
complete	1. the whole with nothing missing. 2. to finish absolutely.
composition	a piece of writing or music.
computer	a machine that solves problems.
comrade	a true friend: a companion.
conceal	to hide from other people.
conceit	pride: vanity.
concern	1. to feel worry about something. 2. to be connected with.
concert	music played in front of people.
conclude	to finish: to bring to an end.
conclusion	the finish: the end.
condition	state. The house was in a poor **condition.**
conduct	how we behave.
conduct	to guide. The **conductor** was collecting the fares.
cone	1. the fruit of the fir tree. 2. a shape that is round at the bottom and pointed at the top.
confess	to own up.
confide	to trust in.
conjuror	a magician: one who can do tricks with his hands.
connect	to join together.
conquer	to win: to beat the others.
conscious	awake: knowing what is happening.
consent	to agree to.
consider	to think very carefully.
constable	a policeman.
construct	to build: to put together the different parts.
contain	to have inside: to hold.
container	a box, jar, chest or bag in which things may be stored. The oil was in a metal **container.**
content	quite pleased: satisfied with things as they are.
contents	what an object contains: what is inside an object.
contest	a struggle to find the best or the winner: a competition.
continent	one of the large land masses, like Europe, America, Australia, Asia, Africa.

continue	to go on with: to go on: to last.
control	to guide: to keep steady.
convenient	suitable. The time was not **convenient.**
convent	the building in which nuns live their holy life.
convey	to carry something from one place to another.
cook	to make food ready to eat by heating it. Mother uses a gas **cooker.**
cool	not quite cold.
copper	a reddish-brown metal.
copy	to imitate: to do the same as somebody else. We were **copying** from the book.
cord	a piece of thick string or thin rope.
core	the middle part: the place where we find the seeds in an apple or a pear.
cork	1. a light substance that is made from the bark of a tree. 2. a stopper for a bottle.
corn	1. the seeds of grain used as food. 2. a sore place on the foot.
corner	where two roads, lines or walls meet.
corpse	a dead body.
correct	quite right: true.
corridor	a narrow, covered passage which joins rooms.
cost	how much we must pay to buy something.
costly	costing very much. The lady was wearing **costly** jewels.
cosy	1. snug: comfortable and warm. 2. the cover for a teapot.
cot	a baby's bed with sides: a crib.
cottage	a small country house.
cotton	thread which is used for sewing and which may be woven to make cloth.
couch	a sofa or settee.
cough	a noisy rush of air from the chest and lungs through the mouth and nose.
count	1. to number in the proper order: to add up. 2. a nobleman. The **Count** and **Countess** were walking together.
counter	1. a table over which things are served in a shop. 2. a small disc used by children in reckoning and in playing games.
country	1. the whole of a land, like England, Scotland or Wales. 2. the part of a land which is away from towns.
county	a part of a country. Surrey and Lancashire are **counties.**
couple	two of anything.
coupon	a ticket which can be changed for something of value.
courage	great bravery.

course	a track such as a **racecourse** or a **golfcourse**. '**Of course** we shall come' means:— '**Certainly** we shall come'.
court	1. a piece of land on which games are played: a **tennis court**. 2. the important people who travel with a king or queen. 3. a place where people are tried.
cousin	the child of an uncle or aunt.
cover	anything placed over something else to hide it.
cow	the name given to some female animals.
coward	a person who runs away from danger.
crab	an eatable shellfish found in or near the sea.
cracker	1. something that explodes with a 'crack'. 2. a kind of biscuit.
cradle	a rocking bed for a baby.
craft	1. cleverness in making things with our hands. 2. a boat.
crafty	not able to be trusted: cunning. A fox is a **crafty** animal.
crag	a rock that juts out from the side of a hill or cliff.
crash	a loud noise made by something breaking.
crawl	1. to move slowly on the hands and knees keeping close to the ground. 2. a stroke used when swimming.
crayon	a coloured chalk made of wax.
crazy	not sensible: foolish: mad.
cream	the thicker liquid found on the top of milk.
creature	a person, animal or insect that is alive.
credit	1. good character. 2. honour.
creek	the place where a tiny stream runs into the sea.
creep	1. to move on the stomach, or on hands and knees. 2. to move very quietly and carefully, bending forward.
crescent	part of the edge of a circle: rounded: the same shape as the new moon.
cress	a tiny vegetable used in salads.
crest	the top of anything, especially the top of a wave.
crew	the people who do the work on a ship or an aircraft.
crib	a baby's bed: a bed made in a manger.
cricket	1. a game played with a ball, bat and stumps. 2. a tiny insect which chirps and which often lives near to fireplaces.
crime	breaking the law.
criminal	a person who breaks the law.
crimson	a deep red colour

crocodile	a large and dangerous land and water animal found in hot countries.
crocus	a small garden bulb which flowers early in the spring.
crook	1. a person who commits a crime: a criminal. 2. a shepherd's stick with a hook at one end.
crop	1. plants which are grown for food. 2. the harvest which is gathered.
cross	1. anything shaped like a 'X' or +. 2. to move from one side to the other as we do over a road. 3. angry.
crow	1. a large, black bird which has a loud, rough cry. 2. the noise made by a cockerel.
crowd	a large number of people all together in one place: a multitude.
crown	1. the special costly head-dress of a king and queen. 2. the top of an object such as a person's head or a hill.
cruel	unkind: without pity. **Cruelty** to animals should not be allowed.
cruise	a long journey by boat or aeroplane.
cruiser	a war ship.

crumb	a tiny piece of bread or cake.
crush	to press together very tightly: to squash.
crust	the hard outside part of anything, especially of bread.
cry	1. to call out. 2. to weep. The children were **crying.**
cub	a young fox or wolf.
cuckoo	a bird which lays its eggs in other birds' nests.
cuddle	to take into the arms and hug tightly.
culprit	a person who is guilty of doing something wrong.
cultivate	to dig or plough land so that crops will grow.
cunning	crafty: not able to be trusted: clever but sly.
cup	a drinking vessel fitted with a handle.
cupboard	shelves for storing things with doors to hide the shelves. The plates were placed in the **cupboard.**
curb	to stop somebody or something from doing something: to hinder.
cure	to make somebody better when he has been ill: to heal.
curious	1. strange: unusual. 2. keen to know.
curls	hair which is combed into rings.

currant a small, dried grape often used in puddings and cakes.

current quickly moving air or water. Bathing was not allowed because of the strong **current.**

curtain a cloth which hangs in front of or beside a window or a stage.

curtsy to bow as a lady does by bending the knee. This word may also be spelt 'curtsey'.

curve a bend: any part which is not straight.

cushion a pillow which is often used on a chair.

custard boiled milk and eggs sweetened.

custom what is usually done: what usually happens.

customer a person who wishes to buy something that is for sale. The **customer** walked into the shop.

cut to open or to divide with something sharp such as a knife or scissors.

cutlery knives, forks and spoons.

cycle a machine with wheels such as a **bicycle** or a **tricycle.**

cygnet a young swan.

D

dab to touch lightly: to pat without rubbing: to clean gently with a sponge or a damp cloth.

dad father.

daffodil a yellow spring flower grown from a bulb.

dagger a pointed knife with a short blade, sharp on both sides.

daily each day.

dainty light on the feet: not clumsy. The girls danced **daintily.**

dairy 1. a shop where milk, butter, eggs and cheese are sold.
2. a place where butter and cheese are made from milk and cream.

dais a small, raised platform often found in a large room such as a school hall.

daisy a tiny flower which has a yellow centre and white petals.

dale a valley.

dam a wall built to hold back water.

damage when something has been harmed.

dame a lady, usually elderly.

damp slightly wet.

damsel a girl: a young lady.

damson a fruit like a small plum, dark purple in colour.

dance to move lightly on the feet to music: a **dancing** party. The girl was a clever **dancer.**

dandelion a yellow, wild flower.

danger	peril: harm: something that can hurt us. To cross the road without looking is **dangerous.**
dangle	to wave up and down: to swing loosely.
dare	to take a risk. To climb the cliff was a **daring** act.
dark	with no light. As clouds gathered, the sky began to **darken.**
darling	someone we love dearly.
darn	to mend a hole in something by passing threads over and under each other.
dart	1. to move very quickly. 2. a short length of pointed metal.
dash	1. to rush from place to place. 2. a very short line.
date	1. the day, month and year when something takes place. 2. a fruit grown on a palm called a date palm.
daughter	a girl child.
dawdle	to do something so slowly that time is wasted.
dawn	daybreak: the light given by the sun when it rises.
day	1. twenty-four hours. 2. the time between sunrise and sunset. In summer there are many hours of **daylight.**

dazed	when we are stunned so that we do not really know what we are doing.
dazzle	to blind for a moment because of a bright light in the eyes.
dead	no longer alive. We read of his **death** in the newspaper.
deadly	able to cause death. The natives were using a **deadly** poison.
deaf	not able to hear easily. The noise of the gunfire **deafened** us.
dealer	a person who buys and sells things.
dear	1. much loved by someone. 2. very costly to buy.
debt	what we owe to someone.
decay	to rot away.
deceit	when we mislead others by lies. The thief tried to **deceive** the police.
decent	proper: respectable.
decide	to make up our minds about what we should do.
decimal	a way of working fractions in tens or tenths.
decision	when we decide what to do.
deck	the floor of a boat, an aeroplane or a bus.
declare	to state firmly: to say what we intend to do.
decline	to say that we do not wish to do something.

decorate to make something more pretty.
At Christmas time, we hang up **decorations.**

decrease to make something smaller.

deed an action: something that we do on purpose.

deep far down, usually in water: far inside.

deer a fast-running, timid animal, with horns.

defeat to beat in game or battle.

defend to protect ourselves: to guard others.

definite sure: certain.

defy to refuse openly to do as we are told: to refuse to obey an order.

delay to put off doing something for a while.

deliberate something done on purpose.
It was worked out very **deliberately.**

delicious giving a pleasant taste when we eat it.

delight pleasure: joy.

deliver 1. to bring: to carry.
2. to make free.

deluge a very heavy fall of rain.

demand to ask for something which we think we should have.

demolish to pull down: to destroy.

demonstrate to show clearly to other people how something should be done.

den the place where an animal eats and sleeps: the animal's lair.

denial 1. when we say that we have not done something, often something wrong.
2. when we say that something is not true.

dense 1. very thick indeed: too thick to see through.
2. stupid.

dent a hollow caused by a blow or knock.

dentist a person who looks after our teeth.

deny to say firmly that we have not done something.

depart to go away: to leave.
The **departure** of the train was announced.

depend to rely on somebody or something to help us.

deposit to place something in a certain place.

depot a place where things are stored: a storehouse.

depress 1. to press something down.
2. to make people feel sad.

depth how deep something is.

derail to make a train leave the rails.

descend to go down: to come down.
The miners began the **descent** of the mine.

c

describe	1. to say how something or someone looks. 2. to give an account of. We were asked to give a **description** of the scene.
desert	to leave when we promised to stay. They **deserted** their friends when trouble came.
desert	a place where nothing grows because of great cold or the lack of rain.
deserve	to earn something good by doing something well.
design	1. a plan or drawing. 2. a drawing made to decorate.
desire	to have a very great wish for something.
desk	a writing table.
desolate	with no living things there: lonely.
despair	to lose hope: to give up hope.
destination	the place to which we are going or to which something has been sent.
destroy	to do away with: to break to pieces.
destroyer	a small fast-moving warship.
detest	to hate: to dislike greatly.
develop	1. to make something become clearer. 2. to grow.
devour	to eat greedily.
dew	drops of water found on the ground in the early morning.

diagram	a sketch or drawing.
dial	1. the face of an object such as a clock. 2. the numbers and letters on a telephone.
dialect	how people speak in a certain district.
diamond	a precious stone which is often used in rings.
diary	a book in which we write what happens each day.
dictate	to tell others what to do. A man who rules alone is a **dictator.**
dictionary	a book which contains a list of words and their meanings, arranged in alphabetical order.
die	to stop living. When frosts come, flowers are **dying.**
diet	the sort of food we eat.
differ	1. not to agree with. 2. to be unlike each other. I went a **different** way from you. There was no **difference** between the two cars.
difficult	not easy to do or to understand. I asked him to help me out of my **difficulty.**
dig	to turn soil over.
digest	to take food into the body through the stomach.

dim   very poorly lit: faint: not easy to see.

dimple   a tiny hollow on the face.

din   a great noise of many things together.

dine   to eat dinner.

dinghy   a small rowing boat.

dinky   small and attractive.

dinner   a main meal.

dint   a hollow made by a knock.

dip
1. to place into a liquid for a short time.
2. to slope downwards.

direct
1. the shortest and quickest way.
2. to tell somebody which way to go.
   We lost our **direction.**

directly   at once: without waiting.
I shall follow you **directly.**

directory   a book containing a list of names and addresses.

dirk   a small dagger.

dirty   not clean: soiled.

dis - - -   The letters 'dis' in front of a word often make the word have the opposite meaning. This will be noticed in some of the words which follow.

disagree   not to agree with.

disappear   to go out of sight: to vanish.

disappoint   to make somebody sorry because they have been let down.
We were **disappointed** when we saw the rain.

disarm   to take weapons from other people.

disaster   a terrible event, happening or accident.

disc   something like a penny which is round and flat. The word may also be spelt 'disk'.

discover   to find out about: to find for the first time.
Captain Cook **discovered** many new lands.

discuss   when several people talk about something.
We had a **discussion** on what to do next.

disease   an illness: a form of sickness.

disgrace   shame: something to be very sorry about.

disguise   to change our appearance by altering the face and clothes.

dish
1. a shallow bowl.
2. the sort of food that is served at a meal.

dislike   not to like: to object to.

dismal   not bright: dreary: not attractive.

dismiss   to send somebody away.

dispatch   to send off letters, parcels or goods.

display   to show to other people in a very special way.

dissolve   to vanish into water so that it can no longer be seen. Salt will **dissolve** in water.

distance
1. somewhere far away.
2. the space between two points or places.

distant	far away.
distinct	quite clearly seen or heard.
distress	great trouble, sorrow or unhappiness.
district	a part of a country or a town.
disturb	1. to upset or to worry somebody. 2. to meddle with and interfere.
disturbance	a trouble: an upset.
ditch	a trench filled with water.
divan	a low bed.
dive	to jump in head first.
divide	to share between: to split up. We are taught how to do **division** sums.
dizzy	unsteady: when we feel as though we are spinning round.
dock	1. the place where boats are loaded and unloaded. 2. the place where a prisoner stands in a police court.
doctor	a person who looks after our health.
dodge	to move quickly from one side to the other.
dog	a tame, four-legged animal.
doll	a toy which looks like a baby or child.
dollar	a form of money used in some countries, such as America and Canada.
donkey	a four-legged, long-eared animal often seen at the seaside.
doom	what is going to happen to us: our fate.
door	an entrance to a room or a building.
dormitory	a large room containing several beds.
dormouse	a type of wild mouse which sleeps during the winter.
dose	the amount of medicine we should take at one time.
dot	a tiny mark such as we could make with a pencil point.
double	1. to multiply by two. 2. to fold in two.
doubt	not to be sure: to question.
dough	the mixture of flour and water ready to be made into bread.
dove	a gentle bird like a pigeon.
down	1. lower: below. 2. soft hair or feathers.
doze	to sleep lightly so that we wake easily.
dozen	twelve. 12.
drab	dull: dismal: not attractive.
drag	to pull something along that is too heavy to lift.
dragon	a frightening monster.
drain	to take water away from something.
drains	the pipes which take the dirty water from buildings.
drama	1. a play which keeps us interested. 2. an exciting happening.
draper	a person who sells things made of cloth.

draught	1. a sharp wind. 2. a cold stream of air entering a warmer room.
draw	1. to sketch. 2. to pull. The **drawer** contained many useful things.
dray	a four-wheeled cart.
dread	to fear very much.
dream	'seeing' things when we are asleep.
dreary	dull: lonely: miserable.
dredger	a boat which cleans out the mud from the bottom of rivers.
drench	to soak through with water.
dress	1. the clothes we wear. 2. a light frock worn by girls and ladies. 3. to put on our clothes.
dressing	bandages or plaster placed over a wound to keep it clean.
drift	1. snow blown into a deep pile. 2. to move with the tide or with the wind.
drill	1. a tool for making holes. 2. exercises done with arms and legs. 3. to make a hole.
drink	to swallow liquids.
drip	when drops of water fall from something.
drive	1. to make a vehicle like a car, move in the way we wish it to go. 2. a private road to a house.
drizzle	light rain falling gently.

droop	to hang down loosely.
drop	1. one tiny spot of liquid. 2. to fall from a height.
drown	not to be able to breathe under water: to die under water.
drum	a musical instrument which is played by beating with a stick.
dry	not wet or even damp.
duchess	the wife of a duke.
duck	1. a common water bird with webbed feet. 2. to put the head under water and bring it up again quickly.
duel	a fight between two people armed with the same sort of weapons.
duke	a nobleman of high rank.
dull	1. not bright. 2. not clever.
dumb	unable to speak.
dungeon	a prison below the ground.
during	as long as something lasts.
dusk	the light at the time of nightfall: sunset.
dust	tiny specks of dirt.
duster	a cloth to remove dust.
duty	something that we should do.
dwarf	a tiny person.
dwell	to live in a certain place.
dwindle	to become less and less.
dye	to make something a certain colour by placing it in a special liquid.

E

each	every one by itself.
eager	very keen.
eagle	a large wild bird found among the mountains.
ear	1. the part of the head with which we hear. 2. where the seed is found in the corn plant.
earl	a nobleman: a man of title.
early	1. before the time fixed. They arrived **earlier** than usual. 2. long ago.
earn	to work for money. The man was paid the wages he had **earned.**
earnest	sincere: serious.
earth	1. the world in which we live. 2. the soil in which things grow.
earthquake	when the earth's surface shakes. The town was shaken by a violent **earthquake.**
earwig	a small insect.
easel	a frame which is on legs and on which we can place a board.
east	the direction from which the sun rises.
easy	simple to do: not difficult to understand. The correct answer was **easily** found.
eat	to bite and swallow food.
eaves	the edges of the roof of a building overhanging the walls.
echo	the same sound which comes back to us in an empty place. Sound often **echoes** in an empty house.
edge	the rim: the border.
editor	a person who prepares a book or a paper before it is printed.
educate	to teach other people. Our **education** takes place at school.
eel	a snake-like fish.
effect	the result: what is found when something has been done.
effort	a great try: the use of all our strength in trying to do something.
egg	the object from which fish and birds are hatched.
eiderdown	a padded bed cover filled with down.
eight	8. a number, one more than seven.
eighteen	18. a number, two nines.
eighty	80. a number, eight tens.
either	one or the other of two people or things.
elastic	a material that will stretch and go back to its own length.

elbow	the joint in the centre of the arm.
elder	1. the older one of two persons. 2. a tree noted for its berries.
elect	to choose somebody by voting. We hold an **election** to pick our school captain.
electric	using electricity.
electricity	a power used to give us light and heat and to drive machines.
elephant	a large animal with a trunk and two tusks.
elevator	1. a rising platform: a lift. 2. the part of an aircraft which makes it climb or dive.
eleven	11. a number, one more than ten.
elf	a small fairy.
elm	a large tree.
else	otherwise: besides.
embark	to go on board a ship or an aeroplane.
embrace	to hold in the arms to show love and affection.
embroider	to decorate material by needlework or sewing. The tablecloth was **embroidered** with flowers.
emerald	a green precious stone.
emerge	to come out and be seen.
emigrate	to leave one country to go to live in another.
emperor	a ruler: a king: a monarch.
empire	many countries which are all under the same ruler.
employ	to give work to someone and to pay them. The man asked for **employment.**
empress	a woman ruler or a queen.
empty	with nothing at all inside. We noticed the **emptiness** of the cave.
enamel	a smooth hard coating of paint which dries bright and shiny.
enclose	1. to place inside. 2. to surround by a fence or wall.
end	1. the last part of something. 2. to finish.
enemy	the person or people we are fighting against.
energy	lively movement: power.
engine	a machine which supplies power and may be worked by steam, electricity, oil or gas.
engineer	a man who looks after machines.
enjoy	to like doing something very much.
enormous	very large: of great size: very big indeed.
enough	sufficient: as many as are needed.
enter	to go into or to come into.
entertain	to amuse: to make people happy by doing something. A children's **entertainment** was held at school.

entire	the whole thing: complete. He said that it was **entirely** his own fault.
entrance	the place where we enter: the way in.
entry	1. an entrance. 2. an item written on a list or in a book.
envelope	the cover in which a letter is placed.
envy	to be jealous of somebody: to wish you could have what somebody else has. She was **envious** because she was not chosen.
equal	the same as: just as good as.
equator	an imaginary line round the earth half-way between the North and South Poles.
ere	before: sooner than.
erect	1. perfectly upright. 2. to build something.
err	to make a mistake.
errand	a short journey to take a message or to fetch something.
error	a mistake: a blunder.
escape	to get away: to find a way out.
estate	1. a large piece of land belonging to one person. 2. a number of houses and shops built in one place.
eternal	lasting for ever.
even	1. equal. 2. the time of evening.
evening	the time between tea-time and sunset.

event	an important happening.
ever	always: at all times.
evergreen	a plant that does not shed its leaves in the winter.
every	each one of many.
evident	easy to see: plain.
evil	wrong-doing: sin.
ewe	a female sheep.
exact	absolutely correct: quite right. It was **exactly** three o'clock.
examine	to test: to check. Each term we have an **examination.**
example	a good pattern which we should follow.
excel	to be better than others. He did **excellent** work.
except	apart from: leaving out.
exchange	1. to change for something else. 2. a main telephone centre.
excite	to thrill. There was great **excitement** at the football match.
exclaim	to shout out suddenly.
excursion	a journey for pleasure.
excuse	1. a reason for not doing what we should have done. 2. to forgive.
execute	1. to carry out an order. 2. to put to death. The king was put into prison to await his **execution.**

exercise
1. movement such as walking and running.
2. to practise often.

exert
1. to move smartly.
2. to make a great effort.

exhibit
to put on display for others to see.
We went to the **exhibition** of children's work.

exile
away from one's own country.

exist
to live: to be.

exit
the way out: the door by which we leave.

expand
to grow larger: to spread out.

expect
to think something will happen: to look forward to.

expedition
a special journey to a place to find out more about it.

expel
to send away: to drive out.

expense
money we spend: the cost of something we buy.

expert
a person who is very clever at something.

explain
to say clearly how something happened.
We asked for an **explanation.**

explode
to blow to pieces with a loud noise.
We heard an **explosion** in the distance.

explore
to search a place thoroughly to find out more about it.

explosive
1. something which will explode.
2. likely to explode.

export
to send goods out of the country.

expose
to uncover.

express
1. to state clearly.
2. travelling more quickly than usual.

extend
to stretch: to make larger.

extra
1. in addition to.
2. more than is required.

extreme
1. farthest away.
2. very great indeed.

eye
1. the part of the head with which we see.
2. the hole in a needle.

F

fable
a story that is made up to teach us a lesson.

face
1. the front part of the head.
2. the front of an object.
3. to turn towards something.

fact
something that is absolutely true.

factor
a number that will go exactly into another number.

factory
a place where goods are made by machinery.

fade
1. to become dim: to become fainter.
2. to begin to grow weaker and to wither.

fail
not to do something that we should do.
I **failed** to help the blind man.
The lights went out because of the electricity **failure.**

faint	1. not clear: not easy to see.
	2. to lose one's senses and become unconscious.
fair	1. lightly coloured in appearance: not dark: blonde.
	2. just and honest.
	3. an open-air entertainment.
	4. halfway between good and poor. My mark in the examination was **fair**.
fairy	a tiny person with magic power.
faith	belief in somebody or something.
faithful	true: reliable. The dog had been a **faithful** friend.
fall	to drop: to become lower.
false	1. not true: not real.
	2. not able to be trusted.
falter	to stumble: to move unsteadily.
fame	importance: becoming well known because of what we have done.
	The man became **famous** after his brave act.
family	all the relatives together.
famine	being without food for a long time.
famished	very hungry indeed.
fan	a machine which makes a draught or wind.
fancy	1. to wish: to desire to have something.
	2. to think that we can see something.
	3. decorated.
fang	a long, sharp tooth on some animals and snakes.

far	not near: distant: a long way off.
fare	1. the sum of money paid for a journey by land, sea or air.
	2. to manage. We **fared** very well on the journey.
farewell	goodbye. We waved **farewell** at the station.
farm	land used for growing crops and rearing animals.
farther	at a greater distance away.
farthest	at the greatest distance away.
fashion	1. up-to-date dress.
	2. to make.
fast	1. at great speed.
	2. a time without food.
	3. not able to move. When we leave a field, we should **fasten** the gate.
fastener	something that prevents things from moving or from coming undone.
fat	1. very big all round: not thin.
	2. the greasy part of meat.
fate	what is going to happen or is likely to happen in the future.
father	the man parent: dad.
fathom	a measure of the depth of water.
fault	1. a flaw. A **fault** was found in the engine.
	2. a mistake. It was my **fault** that we were late.

favour	1. a kindness. 2. to prefer.
favourite	the one that we like better than any of the others. She was a great **favourite** with all her friends.
fear	to be afraid of: to be frightened of something that may happen. There was a **fearful** storm.
feast	a banquet: a rich meal.
feat	something that has been done which needed cleverness or bravery.
feather	the covering of birds.
fee	money paid for something done.
feeble	weak: with no strength.
feed	to eat food.
feel	to touch something with any part of the body.
fellow	a man who is a friend.
felon	one who breaks the law.
felt	thick, woolly cloth.
female	a girl or a woman.
feminine	concerning girls or women.
fence	1. a barrier round land to mark the edge or to stop animals from escaping. 2. to fight with swords.
fender	a metal kerb round the fire-place.
fern	a plant which has feathery leaves but no flowers.
ferry	a boat which carries people and cars across water.

fertile	fruitful: suitable for growing crops.
festival	an enjoyable display for a special occasion.
fetch	to go and get: to bring back what we were sent for.
fever	a disease which makes the body hot. She was kept in bed with a **feverish** cold.
few	not many: a small number.
fiddle	a violin.
fidget	to be restless: to wriggle about.
field	a piece of land that is enclosed by a hedge, fence or wall.
fierce	violent: wild: savage.
fifteen	15. a number: ten and five added together.
fifty	50. a number: five tens.
fig	a fruit shaped rather like a pear and grown in hot lands.
fight	a struggle or battle between two or more people.
figure	1. a number used in arithmetic. 2. an object and its shape. The **figure** of a boy came out of the fog.
file	1. an instrument with a rough edge used to rub away wood or metal. 2. a line of people one behind the other.

fill to make something full.

film
1. a very thin covering: a **film** of ice.
2. a substance on which photographs are taken.
3. to take photographs of things that are moving.
4. a story shown in a cinema.

fin the part of a fish which makes it able to swim.

final the end: the last.
Saturday was the **final** day of our holiday.

finch a small bird.

find to discover.

fine
1. when the weather is pleasant.
2. very good: excellent.
3. very thin.
4. money paid as a punishment for breaking the law.

finger the separate part at the end of the hand.

finish to complete: to end something.

fir an evergreen tree which bears cones.

fire
1. to shoot a gun.
2. burning: when something burns.
The **fireplace** holds the fire.

firm
1. without changing: fixed.
2. a business.

first at the very beginning: with nobody in front.

fish an animal which lives in water.

fist the hand and fingers closed together.

fit
1. in good health: well and strong.
2. suitable.

five 5. a number, four and one added together.

fix
1. to make quite firm.
2. a difficulty which was not expected.

flag
1. a banner: a cloth made of special colours.
2. to become weak and weary.

flake a small piece: a piece shaved off.

flame tongues of fire which come from something that is burning.

flannel heavy, soft, woollen cloth.

flap
1. a piece that hangs down such as the **flap** of a pocket.
2. to move in the same way as a bird moves its wings.

flare to blaze up suddenly.

flash a beam of light which comes and goes quickly.

flat
1. level.
2. a set of rooms on one floor.
3. below the correct note in music.

flavour the taste of something.

flaw a fault: a weak place.

flax a plant grown for its stalk which is used to make linen.

flee	to go away quickly: to run from trouble or danger.
fleece	the sheep's coat of wool.
fleet	a number of ships together.
flesh	the soft part of the body which covers the bones.
flight	what we do when we fly: a **flight** in an aeroplane.
flinch	to draw back because of pain or fear.
fling	to throw something far away from us.
flint	1. very hard stone. 2. the part that makes the spark in a cigarette lighter.
float	to stay on the surface of water without sinking.
flock	1. a number of animals of the same sort together. 2. to gather together.
flog	to beat hard with a stick or a whip.
flood	when water overflows from rivers and lakes on to roads and fields.
floor	the part of a room on which we walk.
florist	a person who sells flowers.
flour	wheat which has been crushed into a powder which is used to make bread.
flow	to glide along like running water.
flower	a blossom on trees and plants.
flute	a musical wind instrument which is made of wood.
flutter	the moving of a bird's wings. The birds **fluttered** in the tree tops.
fly	1. to move through the air. 2. an insect with wings.
foal	a young horse.
foam	froth on the top of water.
foe	an enemy: those who are against us.
fog	air which is thick with mist and smoke. The airport was closed as the day was **foggy**.
fold	1. a place where sheep are kept for safety. 2. to double over. Mother **folds** sheets to keep them tidy.
folk	people.
follow	1. to go after: to come after. 2. to be able to understand what we are told.
folly	stupid behaviour.
fond	'to be fond of' somebody means 'to like them very much.'
food	what we eat and drink.

fool	1. a person who behaves stupidly. 2. to make somebody seem stupid.
foot	1. the part of the body on which we stand. 2. a measure of length.
footwear	boots and shoes.
forbid	to refuse to allow: to tell somebody not to do something.
force	1. strength. 2. to make somebody do something.
ford	a shallow place where a river can be crossed on foot or in a motor car.
fore	the front part.
forecast	to say what is likely to happen.
forefather	a male ancestor: a grandfather, or one of the family who lived a long time ago.
forehead	the part of the head between the hair and the eyes.
foreign	belonging to another country.
forest	a large area of woodland.
forge	a place where metal is heated and shaped: a blacksmith's workshop.
forget	not to remember.
forgive	to pardon: not to punish somebody although he deserves it.
fork	1. a tool with prongs. A small fork is used for eating and a large fork for digging. 2. where two roads or rivers meet.
form	1. the shape of an object. 2. a bench on which we can sit. 3. a class in a school. 4. a printed paper.
former	the first or front one out of two.
forsake	to leave: to give up.
fort	a strong building defended by soldiers. The rebels began to attack the **fortress.**
fortune	either good or bad luck or chance.
forty	40. a number, four tens.
forward	1. towards the front. 2. to send on.
found	to start something such as a hospital or a school.
fountain	spouts of water thrown into the air.
four	4. a number, two twos.
fourteen	14. a number, ten and four added together.
fowl	a fully grown bird.
fox	a crafty wild animal which looks like a dog.
fraction	a part of anything.
fragment	a small piece from something larger.
frame	a border placed round a picture or a photograph.

fraud	a cheat: a false person.
free	1. able to do as we wish. We had **freedom** to go anywhere on the farm. 2. given away without payment.
freeze	to become solid because of cold: to turn into ice. The lake was **frozen** during winter.
frequent	often happening.
fresh	1. new: newly gathered. 2. not tired: ready and willing to do something.
fret	to worry very much about something.
friend	a companion: somebody that we like and can trust.
fright	sudden fear. They were **frightened** by what they had been told.
frill	a decoration round the edge.
frisk	to skip and jump when playing.
frock	a simple dress of a girl or a woman.
frog	an animal grown from a tadpole.
frolic	to run and jump in play.
from	out of: away.
front	the beginning of something: the first part.
frost	very cold, freezing weather
froth	bubbles on top of water.
frown	to wrinkle the forehead because we are not pleased.
fruit	the part of a plant where the seed is found.

fruitful	1. having much fruit. 2. growing good crops.
fry	to cook in boiling fat in a pan.
fuel	anything that will burn.
fulfil	to carry out and to do what we are expected to do.
full	unable to hold anything more.
fun	happy sport: amusement. The behaviour of the monkeys was **funny**.
fund	a collection of money for something special.
funeral	a burial.
funnel	1. the chimney on a ship or an engine. 2. a tube with a wide mouth.
fur	the soft hairy covering of animals.
furious	wild: very angry.
furnace	a special fire to melt metals.
furnish	to supply things that are needed, like chairs or tables.
furniture	chairs, tables and similar things.
further	at a greater distance.
fuss	worry about small things.
future	the time yet to come.

G

gaberdine	1. a cloth often used to make waterproofs. 2. a coat which is usually waterproof.
gable	the pointed end wall of a building.

gag	something to cover the mouth to prevent a person from speaking.
gain	1. a profit that is made. 2. to get something.
gala	a special event: a festival.
gale	a very strong wind.
gallant	noble: brave.
galleon	a Spanish sailing ship of olden times.
gallery	1. a high platform often with seats in a cinema, theatre or a church. 2. a long room used for showing pictures.
galley	a ship's kitchen where the food is cooked for the crew.
gallon	a measure of liquid.
gallop	the way in which four-legged animals move very quickly.
gamble	to play games for money.
gambol	to play: to frolic: to jump about.
game	1. a sport or pastime. 2. animals which are hunted for sport or food.
gander	a male goose.
gang	a group of people all doing the same work.
gangway	1. a pathway between rows of seats. 2. a bridge which is placed between a ship and a dock.

gaol	a prison. The word may also be spelt 'jail'.
gap	an opening between two objects.
garage	the place where motor-cars are kept or repaired.
garden	land where flowers and plants are grown. The **gardener** was weeding the flower bed.
garland	a wreath of flowers or leaves often worn on or over the head.
garment	any piece of clothing.
garrison	a party of soldiers guarding a town or fort.
garter	an elastic band to hold up stockings.
gas	a vapour such as air.
gash	a long deep cut.
gasp	to breathe very quickly: to pant.
gate	an opening in a wall, usually fitted with a door.
gather	1. to collect together. 2. to pluck flowers.
gay	happy: carefree: merry.
gaze	to look at for a long time: to stare steadily.
gem	a jewel such as a pearl or a diamond.
general	1. usual: often done. We **generally** walk home together. 2. an army commander.

generous	kind: giving away freely.
gentle	not rough: full of care for other people. Mother placed the baby **gently** into the cot.
gentleman	a man who is well mannered.
geography	learning about the earth and its people.
germ	a very small living thing in the blood that often causes illness.
get	1. to obtain. 2. to become.
ghost	the spirit of somebody who is dead.
giant	1. anything that is much larger than usual. 2. a huge bad man in a fairy story.
giddy	dizzy: when everything seems to be going round and round.
gift	a present: something given.
giggle	to laugh in a foolish way.
gild	to cover something with gold.
gill	the means by which a fish breathes.
gilt	gold covering; either paint, or real gold.
ginger	a flavouring used in cooking.
gipsy	a wanderer who belongs to a dark-skinned race of people. The word may also be spelt 'gypsy'.
giraffe	an African wild animal with a very long neck and long legs.
girder	a beam of wood or metal used to hold up a building.
girl	a young woman.
give	to hand over as a present.
glacier	a river of ice which moves very slowly.
glad	happy: pleased: delighted.
gladness	happiness: joy.
glance	1. to look at something and then look away quickly. 2. to hit an object with a blow that glides away.
glare	1. to stare at in anger. 2. to dazzle with a bright light.
glass	1. a hard material through which we can see. 2. a drinking vessel.
gleam	a sudden flash or beam of light.
glee	happiness: fun: joy.
glen	a narrow pretty valley.
glide	to move along very smoothly. I went for a flight in a **glider.**
glimmer	a faint light which can hardly be seen.
glimpse	a very short look: a glance.
glitter	to throw out bright rays or light: to sparkle.
globe	1. an object like a ball. 2. a round ball with a map of the world drawn on it.
gloomy	dull and miserable.
glory	beauty: great fame. The army had won a **glorious** victory.

D

glove   a covering for the hand with a separate place for each finger.

glue   a substance for sticking things together.

glum   looking sad and unhappy.

glutton   a person who eats more than is necessary.

gnash   to grind the teeth together because we are angry or in trouble.

gnat   a tiny insect which has wings and which bites.

gnaw   to wear away by using the teeth.

gnome   an elf: a goblin that is supposed to live under the ground.

go   to move away: to leave.
He **goes** to town by train.

goal   a mark or place to aim at in games such as football and hockey.

goat   a farm animal which has horns and which gives milk.

gobble   to eat greedily and noisily.

goblet   a wide drinking cup.

goblin   an elf: a mischievous fairy.

God   one that is worshipped, above all men.

goddess   a female god.

gold   a yellow precious metal.

golden   1. looking like gold.
2. made of gold.

golf   a game played with special clubs and a small ball.

gong   a piece of metal which makes a loud noise when struck.

good   right: reliable: true.

goodbye   farewell.

goose   a large farm bird which looks like a large duck.

gooseberry   an eatable fruit which grows on a small bush.

gorge   a narrow valley between mountains.

gorgeous   very brilliant: glittering: splendid.

gorilla   a large ape: the largest animal that walks on two feet.

gospel   teachings of Jesus Christ.

gossip   1. a person who carries tales about other people.
2. to talk for a long time.

govern   to rule over a country.
The **governor** had arrived at the island.
Members of Parliament help in the **government** of the country.

gown   a long dress.

grab   to snatch: to grasp quickly.

grace   1. a short prayer before a meal.
2. kindness: gentleness: goodness.
She was **gracious** in all that she did.

gradual   little by little.

grain   1. a tiny piece of sand or soil.
2. the seed of corn.

grammar   the rules which give us the correct use of words.

gramme	a unit of weight.
grand	big: chief: splendid.
grandparent	parent of one's father or mother. **Grandfather, Grandmother.**
granite	a very hard rock often used for buildings and monuments.
grant	1. to permit: to give: to allow. 2. to agree that something is true.
grape	the fruit of the vine, often used to make wine.
grasp	1. to hold in the hand. 2. to understand what we have been told.
grass	the green plant used to feed animals and to make lawns.
grate	1. metal bars and the frame round them. 2. to rub together noisily. 3. where the fire burns in a fireplace.
grateful	thankful: giving pleasure.
grave	1. a burial place in the ground. 2. serious.
gravel	small pieces of stone often found in rivers.
gravity	the pull of the earth.
gravy	the juice that comes from cooked meat.
graze	1. to rub away the skin. 2. to feed from grass.

grease	fat, or thick oil. After repairing his bicycle, the boy's hands were **greasy.**
great	big: important: fine.
greedy	always wanting more: never satisfied. He ate his food **greedily.**
green	a colour: the colour of grass.
greet	to welcome: to show that we are pleased when we see somebody.
grey	a colour which is halfway between black and white.
grief	sorrow: unhappiness: deep sadness.
grim	fierce: stern.
grin	a wide smile.
grind	1. to rub something until it becomes powder. The wheat was **ground** to make flour. 2. to sharpen by rubbing the edge.
grip	to grasp tightly.
grit	sand and small pieces of stone mixed together.
groan	to moan when in trouble.
grocer	a man who sells such things as tea and sugar. The boy was delivering **groceries.**
groom	a man who looks after horses.
groove	a narrow cutting.
gross	a number, twelve dozen, 144.

grotto   a cave or cavern made and decorated by man: an artificial cave.

ground   solid earth: land.

group   a number of people or things together.

grow
1. to raise plants.
2. to become bigger.
   We watched the **growth** of the building.

growl   to show anger by snarling.

grub   an insect such as a caterpillar before it has grown wings or legs.

gruff   having a rough coarse voice.

grumble   to mutter and object: to complain.

grunt   the noise made by a pig.

guard
1. to look after.
2. a man in charge of a train on its journey.
3. one who looks after others.
   Her uncle was the girl's **guardian.**

guess   to say what we think is correct without really knowing.

guest   a welcome visitor.

guide   one who shows the way: one who takes the lead.

guilt   having done something wrong: crime.
   The man was found **guilty** at his trial.

guitar   an instrument which has six strings and which is played by plucking the strings.

gulf
1. a large bay at the seaside.
2. a deep wide chasm.

gull   a sea bird found in large numbers at the seaside.

gulp   to swallow greedily and noisily.

gum
1. something used to stick things together.
2. the part of the mouth from which the teeth grow.

gun   a weapon from which bullets are fired.

gush   to flow out quickly in large amounts.

gust   a sudden wind.

gutter   a channel for water.

guy   a person. Guy Fawkes.

gypsy   a dark-skinned wanderer. The word may also be spelt 'gipsy'.

H

habit
1. a custom: something that we have done so often that we do it without needing to think.
2. special clothes for riding a horse.

haddock   a sea-fish rather like a cod.

hag   an ugly woman who looks dirty and untidy.

haggard   looking old, wild and full of trouble.

hail
1. frozen raindrops.
2. to call to someone: to greet.

hair   grows on the head and the skins of people and animals.

half   one part when we divide something into two equal parts.

hall	1. a large room for meetings.
	2. an entrance passage.
	3. a very large house.
hallow	to make holy.
halo	a ring of light round the head of a holy person or round the sun and moon.
halt	to stop what we are doing: to stand still.
halter	a rope with a head-piece for leading a horse.
halve	to divide into two equal parts.
ham	cooked meat from a pig.
hammer	a tool which may be used to drive in nails.
hammock	a hanging mattress or bed held up by ropes.
hamper	1. a large wooden or cane basket with a lid.
	2. to hinder.
hamster	a small animal like a large mouse.
hand	the part of the body at the end of the arm.
	In **handwork** lessons we make interesting things.
handicap	something that hinders us.
handicraft	making things by hand.
handkerchief	a small piece of cloth for wiping the nose.
handle	1. to touch with the hand.
	2. the part of an article which we take in our hand such as a **brush handle.**

handsome	good looking: tall and well-built.
hang	to fasten up by a cord.
hangar	a shed in which aeroplanes are stored.
hanger	something by which we hang an object such as a **clothes hanger.**
happen	to occur: to take place. We walked to the crowd to see what was **happening.**
happily	gladly.
happiness	joy: pleasure.
happy	contented: glad: pleased.
harbour	a place of shelter for boats.
hard	1. difficult to do.
	2. tough: firm.
hardly	scarcely: only just. We had **hardly** sat down before the train began to move.
hare	an animal like a large rabbit.
hark	to listen.
harm	danger: trouble.
harness	the leather straps which are the reins and bridle for a horse.
harp	a large musical instrument which rests on the floor and which is played by plucking the strings.
harpoon	a spear which is used in catching whales.
harsh	unkind: unjust: rough.
harvest	a crop of food gathered in.
haste	speed: quickness: hurry.
hat	a head covering.

hatch	1. to be born from an egg. 2. to make secret plans. 3. an opening into the deck of a ship.	**hear**	1. to catch the sound of: to listen to. 2. to receive news.
hatchet	a small axe.	**hearse**	a carriage in which a coffin is carried.
hate	to dislike very much: to detest.	**heart**	1. the part of the body which pumps the blood round the body. 2. the centre or most important part of anything.
haul	to drag: to pull. The fishermen were busy **hauling** in their nets.	**hearth**	the part of the floor in front of the fireplace.
haunt	to visit very often.	**heat**	warmth.
haunted	lived in by a ghost. The old house was said to be **haunted.**	**heathen**	someone who does not believe in God.
have	to possess: to own.	**heather**	a small shrub which grows on moorlands.
haven	a harbour: a place of safety.	**heave**	1. to pull strongly. 2. to lift something and then throw it.
havoc	great damage: ruin.	**heaven**	the place where we believe God to be.
hawk	a large bird which attacks and kills smaller birds.	**heavy**	having great weight: not easily lifted.
hay	dried grass. The farmer was building a **haystack.**	**hedge**	bushes used to divide one part from another: a fence made of shrubs.
haze	light mist or thin cloud.	**hedgehog**	a prickly-backed animal which rolls itself into a ball when in danger.
head	1. the part of the body above the neck. 2. the chief person.	**heel**	the back part of the foot.
headache	a pain in the head.	**height**	distance from top to bottom: how tall something is.
heal	to make well again after being hurt or ill: to cure.	**heir**	a man or boy who receives a dead person's property.
health	freedom from illness: fitness. Exercise and games keep us **healthy.**	**heiress**	a girl or woman heir.
heap	a pile: things placed one on top of another.	**helm**	a wheel which is turned to steer a ship.

helmet a covering for the head, often made of something to protect the head.

help to aid: to assist.
The girl was **helpful** to her mother.

helpless without help.

hem an edge of cloth which has been turned over and stitched.

hen a female bird.

hence 1. away from here.
2. from now onwards.

herald a person who announces special happenings.

herb a plant which is used as a medicine or for its flavour.

herd a large number of the same sort of animals together.

here at this place.

hermit one who lives in a lonely place.

hero a man or boy who acts with great bravery.
To rescue the drowning boy was a **heroic** act.
The girl was the **heroine** of the school.

herring a small seafish which is used for food.

hide 1. the skin of an animal.
2. to keep in a secret place.
3. to go where we cannot be found.

high taller than other things.

highway a road which may be used by everybody.

highwayman a man who stopped travellers and robbed them.

hill a low mountain.

hilt the handle of a sword or dagger.

himself he alone.

hinder to prevent: to check.
The snow proved a **hindrance** to us.

hinge a moving joint which allows a door to open and close easily.

hint to suggest.

hip the place where the legs join the body.

hippopotamus a large land and water animal found in Africa.

hire to borrow something for a short time and pay to use it.

hiss to breathe out sharply through the teeth.

history the story of past times.

hit to strike.

hive the home of bees.

hoard to gather together and store in a secret place.

hoarse rough: coarse.

hobby an interesting and useful pastime.

hockey a game played by two teams with curved sticks and a ball.

hoe a tool used for taking out weeds.

hold 1. to keep a grip of.
2. to have inside.
3. the storage part of a ship.

hole an opening: a gap.

holiday a time of rest: a time when we are free from work.

hollow	empty: with nothing inside.
holly	an evergreen bush with sharp-pointed leaves.
holy	godly: free from sin.
home	the place where we live.
homely	simple: plain. The old couple were **homely** people.
honest	able to be trusted: truthful. We knew that we could depend on his **honesty**.
honey	a sweet food made by bees.
honour	good name: respect: fame.
hood	1. a covering to protect the head and shoulders. 2. a cover for a baby's pram or for a motor-car.
hoof	the hard part of the foot of some animals: the **hooves** of a horse.
hook	a bent and pointed piece of metal.
hoop	a ring of wood or metal.
hoot	a call like that of an owl. The **hooter** of a motor-car warns of danger.
hop	1. to jump up and down on one foot. 2. a plant used in making beer.
hope	to wish that something pleasant will happen.
hopeless	impossible: not worth hoping for. The task we were given seemed **hopeless**.
horizon	the line where the sky and the earth seem to touch.
horn	1. hard bone sticking out from the head of an animal. 2. a musical instrument which must be blown to make it play.
horrible	very unpleasant: terrible.
horrid	dreadful: fearful.
horse	a large animal tamed and used by man.
hose	1. a tube through which water will flow. 2. stockings.
hospital	a place where sick people are cared for.
host	1. a large group of people. 2. a man who invites others to his house. We were met at the door by the **host** and **hostess**.
hot	very warm indeed.
hotel	a building where we pay to eat and sleep: an inn.
hound	a dog which is trained to hunt.
hour	a length of time of sixty minutes.
house	a building in which people live.
hovel	a poor, dirty, tumbledown house.
how	in which way.
howl	a long, loud cry: a wail.
hub	the centre part of a wheel.
hug	to hold tightly in the arms.
huge	very large indeed.

hum	1. the noise made **by** bees. 2. to make the sound of a tune without **the** words.
human	connected with men and women.
humble	meek: simple.
humour	fun and happiness.
hump	a lump higher than **the** rest. A camel has one or two **humps** on its back.
hundred	100. a number, ten tens: a century.
hunger	a great need for food. After our long walk, we were **hungry**.
hunt	1. to try to catch wild animals. 2. to look very **carefully** for something.
hurl	to throw far away.
hurrah	a shout for joy.
hurry	to move very quickly: to rush.
hurt	to injure: to damage.
husband	a married man.
hush	quietness: silence.
hut	a small, wooden building.
hyacinth	a flower grown from a bulb.
hymn	a song of praise or thanks to God.

I

ice	frozen water. The motor-cars were skidding on the **icy** road.
iceberg	a hill or a mountain of ice floating on the sea. The ships were warned that an **iceberg** was near.
icicle	a spike of ice hanging downwards. An **icicle** was hanging from the roof of the house.
icing	a coating of sugar for cakes and buns.
idea	a thought: something in the mind.
ideal	just what is needed.
idiot	a person who behaves stupidly.
idle	lazy: not wishing to work.
idol	an image or statue which is worshipped as a god.
igloo	an Eskimo house made of snow blocks.
ignite	to set fire to: to catch fire.
ignorant	not wise: knowing nothing.
ill	not well: in poor health. In winter time, **illness** is common.
ill-treat	to treat badly.
illuminate	to light up. The coloured lights were a pretty **illumination**.
illustrate	to explain something by drawing pictures.
image	1. a figure carved in wood or stone: a statue. 2. something that is exactly like someone else. The girl was the **image** of her mother.
imaginary	something that we imagine: not real.

imagine	to form a picture in the mind.
imitate	to copy: to do the same as somebody else.
immediate	1. near: close. 2. next: following.
immense	large: huge.
imp	a playful, mischievous child.
impertinent	rude to older people.
implore	to ask: to beg.
import	to bring goods from another country into this country.
important	of great value: mattering very much.
imprison	to put into prison.
improve	to make something better: to get better.
inactive	not active: still: idle.
incense	something which smells sweetly when burned.
inch	1. a measure of length. 2. to move very slowly along.
incident	a happening: something that occurs.
incline	a slope: a slant.
include	to put in something with other things.
income	money which is earned or received.
incorrect	not correct: wrong.
increase	to make larger or greater.
indeed	as a matter of fact: really.
independent	able to act alone.
index	a list showing everything that is in a book.
indignant	angry: furious: annoyed.

infant	a baby: a young child.
inform	to tell: to give the news.
inhabit	to live in a certain place.
injure	to hurt: to harm.
ink	a liquid used for writing.
inland	away from the coast.
inn	a hotel: a place where travellers may eat and sleep.
innings	when we bat at cricket or rounders.
innocent	not to blame: not guilty.
inquire	to ask questions.
insane	not in the right mind: mad.
insect	a very small living creature with six legs.
inside	1. the part which is enclosed. 2. within.
insist	1. to demand. 2. to be very firm.
instalment	one part of something that is not yet finished.
instead	in place of.
instruct	to teach. When we go to the swimming bath, we are given **instruction** by an **instructor**.
instrument	1. a tool. 2. something which is made to give out musical sounds.
intelligent	quick to learn: sensible.
intend	to mean to do something.
interest	keen attention.
interfere	to get in the way of: to meddle.
interior	the inside: the part within

interrupt	to stop: to break in when other people are doing something.
interval	a break: a pause.
into	inside: within.
invade	to enter by using force if this is needed.
invent	to make something for the first time.
invert	to turn over: to turn upside down.
invisible	not visible: not able to be seen.
invite	to ask somebody to come.
iris	1. a large flower grown from a bulb. 2. the coloured part of the eye.
iron	1. a hard, strong metal. 2. a tool for pressing clothes.
island	a piece of land with water all round it.
itch	a tickling of the skin.
item	one thing out of a list of many things.
itself	the thing alone.
ivory	hard, white bone from elephants' tusks.
ivy	a climbing evergreen plant.

J

jab	to poke at or to stab at something.
jackal	a wild animal that looks like a dog.
jacket	a short coat.
jail	a prison. The word may also be spelt 'gaol'.
jam	1. a food made from fruit and sugar. 2. not to be able to move because of a crowd. We were held up in a traffic **jam**.
jar	1. a container with an opening at the top. 2. to grate: to make a sound that makes us shudder.
jaw	the lower part of the face: the bones to which our teeth are fixed.
jay	a brightly coloured bird which chatters.
jazz	a form of dance music.
jealous	when we wish we had what others have: envious. She was filled with **jealousy** when she saw what the others had been given.
jeep	a small, powerful motor-car.
jeer	to sneer at: to make rude remarks about something.
jelly	a food made from fruit juice.
jerk	a sudden push or pull.
jersey	a form of clothing that is often knitted.
jest	to joke: to make fun of.
jet	1. a thin stream of water or air. 2. an engine driven by a stream of air passing through special tubes.

jewel	a precious stone. The ring was bought from a **jeweller.** The ladies were wearing beautiful **jewellery.**
jig	a lively dance.
jingle	to tingle: to rattle.
job	work: something to do.
jockey	the rider of a racehorse.
jog	1. to trot. 2. to push.
join	1. to fasten together. 2. to combine with others.
joiner	a man who works with wood: a carpenter.
joint	1. a piece of meat. 2. where two parts are fastened together.
joke	an amusing story.
jolly	happy: lively: merry.
jolt	a sudden jerk or stop.
jot	1. to write down quickly. 2. a tiny piece.
journey	a trip from place to place.
joy	happiness: gladness: glee.
judge	a person who decides who is right or who is wrong. When the trial was over **judgment** was given.
jug	a container for liquids.
juggler	a person who can do clever tricks with balls and clubs.
juice	the liquid of fruit and vegetables. He was eating a **juicy** orange.
jumble	a muddle: many things mixed together.
jump	to spring into the air with both feet off the ground.
jumper	1. one who jumps. 2. a knitted garment worn on the body.
junction	where two or more roads meet or cross.
jungle	a thick, wild forest through which we can hardly move.
junior	younger or lower than the others.
junk	1. rubbish that is of no use to anyone. 2. a Chinese sailing boat.
jury	people who listen to a trial in a police court and decide if a prisoner is guilty.
just	fair: right. The man asked **for justice** to be done.
jut	to stick out from.

K

kangaroo	an Australian animal with long back legs and short front legs.
keel	the bottom part of a boat on which the rest of the boat is built.
keen	eager: anxious to do what should be done.

keep	to hold: to have for oneself.
kennel	a hut in which a dog is kept.
kerb	the border or edge of a path or pavement.
kernel	the centre part of a nut: the part that we eat.
kettle	a container in which we boil water and which is fitted with a handle and spout.
key	a tool to open a lock.
kick	to hit with the foot or toes.
kid	1. a young goat. 2. the leather from a goat's skin.
kidnap	to take and hide a child away from its parents.
kill	to take the life of: to put to death.
kilt	a pleated skirt often worn by men in Scotland.
kilometre	a thousand metres.
kin(dred)	our relatives:— father, mother, brother and so on.
kind	1. sort: type. 2. gentle: good.
kindle	to set fire to: to light.
kindness	gentleness: goodness.
king	a man ruler: a monarch. When his father died, the young king ruled the **kingdom**.
kipper	a smoked herring made ready to eat.
kiss	to touch with the lips.
kitchen	a room where food is cooked.

kite	a light framework covered with material and made ready to fly.
kitten	a young cat.
knead	to mix the dough ready to make bread.
knee	the joint in the middle of the leg. We **kneel** to say our prayers.
knickers	short trousers.
knife	a sharp blade fitted with a handle.
knight	the title given to a man by the King or Queen. **Sir Winston Churchill.**
knit	to weave wool or cotton with needles.
knob	a round handle used on doors and on furniture.
knock	to make a tapping noise. We used the **knocker** on the door.
knot	a fastening made by twisting string or rope.
know	1. to be sure. 2. to remember somebody. His **knowledge** of the town surprised us.
knuckle	a joint of the fingers.

L

label	a paper or card for fastening on to parcels.
labour	work: a job to be done.
lace	1. an open-work pattern of cotton. 2. a strong string.

lack	absence of: being short of something we need.
lad	a boy.
ladder	1. movable steps used for climbing. 2. where the threads or stitches are broken in a stocking.
ladle	a large spoon with a long handle.
lady	a well-mannered woman. She behaved in a **lady-like** way.
lag	to move slowly: to drag behind the others.
lagoon	shallow, calm sea-water in a bay.
lair	a wild animal's den.
lake	a large stretch of water: a large pond.
lamb	a young sheep.
lame	unable to walk properly: limping.
lament	to mourn: to be sad about.
lamp	something made to give a light.
lance	a long thin spear.
land	1. the solid part of the earth. 2. a piece of ground. The squire was the **landlord** of the village.
lane	a narrow road or a wide pathway.
language	the words used by a person or by the people of a country.
lantern	a case in which to carry a light that can be seen.
lap	1. the thighs when we are sitting down. 2. the sound made by a dog when it is drinking.
lapse	a mistake: something not done.
larch	a tree which bears cones and has pointed leaves.
lard	fat used in baking, cooking and frying.
large	big: huge.
lark	a small singing bird which flies high in the sky.
lash	1. to fasten tightly with rope or string. 2. a whip. 3. a small hair on the eyelid.
lass	a girl: a young woman.
lasoo } **lasso** }	a rope with a noose for catching animals.
last	1. at the end: final. 2. to endure.
latch	a fastening for a door or gate.
late	not early: behind time.
lath	a long thin piece of wood.
latter	the second of two.
laugh	the sound we make when we are amused. Sounds of **laughter** were heard at the party.
launch	1. a motor boat. 2. to float a newly-built boat.

laundry	a place where clothing is taken to be washed.
lavatory	a room for washing.
law	a rule to be obeyed by all. We must all behave in a **lawful** manner.
lawn	grass kept cut and tidy.
lawyer	a person who has studied the law.
lay	1. to put down. 2. to produce eggs.
lazy	idle: not wishing to do anything useful.
lead	(say 'led') a heavy metal.
lead	(say 'leed') to guide: to go in front for others to follow.
leader	a guide: the one who goes in front.
leaf	1. part of a tree or plant. The **leaves** of many trees fall in the autumn. 2. a page of a book.
leak	a hole from which gas or liquid can flow out.
lean	1. thin. 2. to put our weight on. 3. to bend towards.
leap	to spring: to jump.
learn	to get to know: to become skilful.
least	the smallest.
leather	an animal's skin which has been tanned ready for use.
leave	to forsake: to go away from.
lecture	a speech which teaches.
ledge	a narrow shelf: something narrow. We climbed along the **ledge** on the cliff to reach the flowers.
leek	a vegetable which is rather like an onion.
left	the opposite to right: the same side of the body as the heart.
leg	1. the limb with which we walk. 2. the corner supports of furniture such as tables.
legend	a story from long ago, sometimes true, sometimes partly true.
leisure	spare time used for hobbies and amusement.
lemon	a yellow, sour-tasting fruit.
lend	to allow somebody to use something for a time.
length	the distance from one end to the other. Mother decided to **lengthen** the dress.
leopard	a fierce wild animal with a spotted skin.
leper	a person suffering from leprosy.
leprosy	a serious and dreadful disease.
less	smaller: not so big.
lesson	something we should learn.

let	1. to allow: to permit. 2. to allow somebody to use a house and pay a rent.
letter	1. a written message sent to somebody. 2. A, B, C, are letters.
lettuce	a vegetable used in salads.
level	the same height all along: flat.
lever	a strong metal bar for lifting things.
liar	a person who purposely does not speak the truth.
liberty	freedom.
library	a place where books are stored. The **librarian** was tidying the books on the shelves.
licence	a paper that gives us permission to do something:— a television **licence**.
license	to allow us to do something. The man must **license** his car.
lick	to wet with the tongue.
lid	a cover that can be taken off.
lie	1. to tell an untruth. 2. to rest in a flat position.
life	the time when we are alive.
lift	1. to raise. 2. a cage or platform that moves from floor to floor in a building.
light	1. brightness. 2. easy to lift: having little weight. Some of the things were taken from the cart to **lighten** it.

lightning	the flashes that we see in the sky in a thunder-storm.
like	1. to be fond of. 2. the same as: similar to.
likely	what we should expect.
lilac	a small tree having sweet-smelling blossom.
lily	a bell-shaped flower grown from a bulb.
limb	1. a part of the body such as an arm or a leg. 2. a branch of a tree.
lime	a white powder made from limestone.
limestone	a greyish-white rock used for building.
limit	the end: as far as we can go.
limp	1. to walk lamely. 2. not firm or straight.
line	1. a narrow mark. 2. a piece of rope or string.
linen	cloth made from flax and used for such things as sheets and table-cloths.
liner	a large passenger boat or aeroplane.
linger	to stay near: not to go far away.
lining	a cloth backing for clothes.
link	a ring in a chain.
linnet	a small singing-bird.
linoleum	a stiff floor-covering often having a printed pattern.
lint	soft cloth used for putting on wounds.
lion	a large, fierce, wild animal: the king of beasts. The **lion** and the **lioness** were guarding their cubs.

lip	1. the front edge of the mouth. 2. the edge or brim of a jug and other containers.
liquid	something that will flow like water or milk.
liquor	anything liquid.
liquorice	a sweet made from a plant root.
list	1. a number of names written one below another. 2. to lean sideways.
listen	to try to hear. We **listened** carefully to what we had to do. He learned quickly because he was a good **listener.**
literature	well-written stories and poems.
litre	a measure of liquids.
litter	1. rubbish lying about. 2. a number of animals born together.
little	small: tiny.
live	1. to dwell. 2. to be alive. The kitten was a **lively** little animal.
livelihood	the means by which we live: work.
liver	a part of the body which helps to use the food that has been eaten.
lizard	a four-footed animal with a long tail and tiny legs.
load	1. a burden. 2. a number of things to be moved about. 3. to make a gun ready for firing.

E

loaf	a piece of baked bread. The boy had the **loaves** in his basket.
loan	1. something that is borrowed or lent. 2. to lend.
lobster	a shell-fish with claws.
local	belonging to the same place.
loch	a lake in Scotland.
lock	1. to fasten something so that only a key will open it. Our clothes were placed in a **locker.** 2. a place in a canal where ships are raised or lowered. 3. a piece of hair.
locomotive	a railway engine.
locust	an insect which is like a grasshopper and which destroys crops.
lodge	1. to pay to stay in a house The man was seeking a **lodging** for the night. 2. a small house at the entrance of a drive leading to a larger house.
loft	1. the top room of a building. 2. the space under the roof of a building.
lofty	very tall: very high.
log	1. part of a tree branch. 2. a ship's diary.
loll	to sprawl or lean lazily.
lone	without anybody else there. The **lonely** house stood beside the lake.

long	1. of great length: not short.
	2. to wish for very much.
look	1. to watch: to see.
	2. a glance.
loom	1. a machine for weaving.
	2. to come into sight slowly, often out of mist or darkness.
loop	a ring of string or rope.
loose	slack: free to move.
	The rope was so tight that we could not **loosen** it.
lop	to cut branches from a tree.
lord	a nobleman.
lorry	a large motor waggon made to carry loads.
lose	1. to be beaten.
	2. to miss.
loss	something that we have lost.
loud	with a great noise.
lounge	1. a sitting room in a house or hotel.
	2. to act lazily.
love	to be very fond of.
	The dog was a **lovable** creature.
lovely	delightful: beautiful.
	The girl was given a **lovely** doll.
low	1. not high: near to the ground.
	2. quiet: hardly able to be heard.
	3. the sound made by cattle.
lowly	meek: simple: mild.
loyal	reliable: true to people who trust us such as our friends.

luck	fortune: chance.
	It was **lucky** that we arrived when we did.
	Luckily it did not rain.
luggage	baggage and trunks containing our belongings when we are travelling.
lull	a pause.
lullaby	a quiet song to send a baby to sleep.
lump	1. a swelling.
	2. a piece of something.
lunar	connected with the moon.
lunatic	a mad person.
lunch	1. the mid-day meal.
	2. a light meal of sandwiches and cake.
lung	the part of the body in the chest where we breathe.

M

machine	an instrument built by man to do work.
	An engine is a clever piece of **machinery**.
mackerel	a sea fish used for food.
mackintosh	a raincoat: a waterproof.
mad	1. insane: very foolish.
	2. angry.
madam(e)	the title of a lady, usually a married woman.
magazine	1. a paper containing stories.
	2. a storage place for explosives.
magic	conjuring: trickery.
	The **magician** was especially clever with his tricks.
magnet	iron or steel which attracts other pieces of iron or steel.

magnify	to make things appear larger.
magpie	a wild bird which is black and white.
maid	1. a girl servant. 2. a girl.
mail	1. letters and parcels sent by post. 2. armour worn by soldiers in olden days.
main	most important: chief.
maize	a corn grown in warm countries.
majesty	the title given to a king or queen.
major	1. an important army officer. 2. the chief: the most important.
make	1. to build: to construct something. 2. to force somebody to do something.
male	man or boy: masculine.
malt	a substance made from barley and used for making beer.
mammoth	1. a large animal of long ago. 2. huge.
man	a male person.
manage	1. to be able to do something. 2. to take charge of something. He was the **manager** of the shop.
mane	the long hair on an animal's neck.
manger	an animal's feeding box in a stable.
mangle	a machine with rollers for pressing clothes.
manner	1. the way in which we behave. 2. the way in which a thing is done.
manor	a large country house: the chief house of a village and its land.
mansion	a large house.
mantle	1. a cloak without sleeves. 2. a cover.
manufacture	to make things in a works or factory usually by using machinery.
many	a number of: plenty.
map	the drawing of a district, a country, or the world.
maple	a tree which is like a sycamore tree.
marble	1. a hard stone which can be smoothly polished. 2. a round glass or stone ball with which children play.
march	1. to walk in step with others. 2. a piece of music to which we can walk.
mare	a female horse.
margarine	a food which is often used instead of butter.
margin	a border down the side of a page of a book.
mariner	a sailor.

mark	1. a sign put on to something. 2. a spot or stain. 3. to see and notice.
market	a place where goods are sold and bought.
marmalade	a form of jam made from oranges or lemons.
maroon	a brownish-red colour.
marriage	a wedding.
marry	to take a husband or wife: to wed.
marsh	a bog: wet land: a swamp.
martyr	a person who gives up his life because of what he feels to be right.
marvel	a surprising and amazing happening. The conjuror did a **marvellous** trick.
mascot	a charm: something supposed to bring good luck.
masculine	concerning boys and men.
mask	a covering for the face.
mass	1. a large piece of something. 2. a crowd of people.
massive	very large: huge: enormous.
mast	a pole on a ship used to hold the sails.
master	the chief man: the man in charge.
mat	a small rug.
match	1. a small, thin stick tipped with a mixture which catches fire easily when rubbed. 2. a game between two teams. 3. an equal.
mate	1. a companion: a friend. 2. a sailor.
material	something from which things are made.
matter	1. a substance: what things are made of. 2. to be important.
mattress	a soft bed-covering on which we sleep.
maul	to handle something roughly and to damage it.
mauve	a purple colour.
may	to be possible.
mayor	the chief man in a town.
mayoress	the chief lady in a town.
meadow	a stretch of grassland.
meal	1. the food which we eat at a certain time. 2. flour made from corn.
mean	1. not generous. 2. to intend to do something. We **meant** to call for you this morning.
meaning	an explanation: the reason why something happened.
measles	a disease common among children.
measure	1. to find out how much there is or how many there are. 2. something for finding out how long something is.
measurement	how big something is.
meat	flesh taken from an animal and used as food.
medal	a metal disc given to reward us for what we have done.
meddle	to interfere in matters which are not our business.

medicine	something which we take to make us better when we are not well.
meek	gentle.
meet	1. to come together. 2. to go to see and greet somebody.
melancholy	sad and unhappy.
melody	a tune.
melon	a juicy fruit.
melt	to heat something until it becomes a liquid.
member	a person who belongs to a special group.
memory	the part of the brain with which we remember.
men	males.
menagerie	many animals together on show: a zoo.
mend	to repair: to put right.
mental	done in the mind without writing down.
mention	to talk about: to say.
merchant	a man who buys and sells.
mercy	pity: forgiveness.
merry	gay: happy: joyful. We ran into the sea **merrily.**
mess	1. many things mixed together: a jumble. 2. a group of people who eat together regularly.
message	news sent from one person to another.
metal	materials such as iron, steel, gold, silver and brass.
meter	a machine for measuring such things as gas or electricity.
method	the way in which something is done.

metre	a measurement of length.
mew	the noise made by a cat.
microphone	a machine which picks up sounds and makes them louder.
microscope	an instrument to magnify small things.
mid	the middle: the centre. The taxi arrived at **mid-day.** The boy stood in the **middle** of the ring.
midst	the middle: the centre.
might	strength: power. The man gave the metal a **mighty** blow.
mild	1. gentle: not rough. 2. not too cold. The weather is **mild** today.
mile	a measurement of distance.
milk	a white liquid given by animals to feed their young. The young child was given **milky** food.
mill	1. a place where corn is ground into flour. The **miller's** clothes were covered with a white dust. 2. a factory.
millimetre	a thousandth of a metre.
million	1 000 000. a thousand thousands.
millionaire	a person who is very rich indeed.
mince	to cut into tiny pieces.
mind	1. to object to something. 2. the brain. 3. to look after something or somebody.

mine	1. belonging to me. 2. a place from which minerals are dug from the earth.
mineral	things such as rock and coal which are dug out of the earth.
mingle	to mix with.
minister	1. a clergyman: a priest. 2. an important member of the government.
minor	1. the younger one. 2. the smaller one.
mint	1. the place where money is made. 2. a herb used in cooking.
minus	less than: without: the sign —.
minute	a length of time of sixty seconds.
minute (say 'my nute') very small.	
miracle	a remarkable event which we did not think could have happened.
mirror	a looking glass.
mirth	happiness: joy: laughter.
mischief	silly pranks: stupid actions.
mischievous	always in mischief.
miser	a person who has plenty of money yet tries not to spend any.
miserable	full of sadness.
misery	unhappiness: sorrow.
mislead	to lead astray.
miss	1. not to see: not to succeed. 2. a young lady.
mission	a special task.
mist	a fog: a haze.

mistake	a fault: an error.
mistress	the chief lady: the lady in charge.
mitten	a glove with one place for all the fingers.
mix	to mingle things by stirring them together.
mixture	things mixed together.
moan	a groan: a sound of pain.
moat	a ditch round a castle to keep it safe from attack.
mob	an unruly crowd of people trying to do harm to others.
mock	to imitate: to make fun of somebody.
model	1. a copy of something. 2. a pattern to be followed.
modern	up-to-date.
module	an independent part of a space craft.
moist	damp. We must **moisten** a stamp before we stick it on a letter. The ground in the early morning was covered with **moisture.**
mole	a small furry animal which burrows under the ground.
moment	a short space of time.
monarch	a king or queen: an emperor or empress: a ruler.
monastery	a building in which monks live.
money	cash: coins: banknotes.
mongrel	a dog of two or more breeds.
monitor	a child who helps the teacher.
monk	a man who spends his life in religion and who lives in a monastery

monkey	a small ape.	**moult**	when a bird sheds its feathers.
monster	a large beast which terrifies us.	**mount**	to climb up.
month	1. one of the twelve parts of a year: **August.**	**mountain**	a high hill.
	2. four weeks.	**mourn**	to be very sad.
	At school, we have a **monthly** test.	**mouse**	a small animal with a long tail.
monument	a statue: something built to remind us of a very important event.	**mouth**	1. the part of the head with which we eat and speak.
mood	temper: how we feel in the mind.		2. where a river enters the sea.
moon	a heavenly body seen in the sky at night.	**move**	to go from one place to another.
moor	1. hills often covered with heather.		We noticed a **movement** behind the bushes.
	2. to fasten a boat by using a rope.	**mow**	to cut corn or grass.
mop	a soft brush used for polishing.	**Mr.**	Mister: the title given to a man.
more	a greater number.	**Mrs.**	Mistress: the title given to a woman who is married.
morning	the part of the day which comes before noon.	**much**	a great quantity.
morsel	a tiny piece of something.	**mud**	wet soil.
moss	a plant which grows on trees and walls.		The path over the field was **muddy.**
most	the greatest number.	**muddle**	a jumble: a mixture.
moth	a flying insect like a butterfly.	**muff**	a covering into which the hands may be placed to keep them warm.
mother	the woman parent.	**muffin**	a thin cake which is rather spongy.
motion	movement.	**muffle**	1. to cover up closely to keep warm.
motor	a driving engine to make things move or turn.		2. to deaden the sound.
	The doctor arrived in his **motor-car.**	**mug**	a large drinking cup used without the saucer.
motto	a saying which should guide or help us.	**mule**	an animal which is cross-bred and is half horse and half donkey.
mould	to make something into the right shape.		

multiply	to make something so many times greater. We are learning how to do **multiplication** sums.
multitude	a large number of people all together.
mumble	to speak so that we cannot be heard easily.
mumps	a painful neck illness common among children.
munch	to eat noisily.
murmur	1. to speak very softly. 2. a low sound.
muscles	the parts of the body which help us to move the limbs.
museum	a building where interesting and ancient things can be seen.
music	pleasing sounds and notes. The **musicians** took their places on the platform.
must	to be forced to do something.
mustard	a paste made from seeds and used for flavouring.
muster	to gather together in order to carry out a plan.
mutiny	a rising against the leader, usually by soldiers or sailors.
mutter	to speak in a low voice.
mutton	the meat from sheep.
muzzle	1. a covering placed over an animal's mouth. 2. the open end of the barrel of a gun.
my	belonging to me. I was told to do it **myself.**
mystery	a problem: something that we cannot understand.

N

nag	1. to grumble about small things: to annoy. 2. a horse.
nail	1. a pointed piece of metal. 2. the horny part of the fingers and toes.
naked	bare: not covered.
name	a word by which someone or something is called.
nanny	1. a female goat. 2. a children's nurse.
nap	a short sleep.
napkin	a small piece of cloth to keep us clean.
narrow	not far across: not wide.
nasty	1. not good to taste. 2. not pleasant to see.
nation	people belonging to one country. The people were dressed in **national** costume. We did not know the man's **nationality.**
native	a person born in a certain country.
nature	1. living things:— people, animals, plants, flowers. 2. how we behave and act. It was **natural** for her to be kind to others.
naughty	badly behaved.
naval	to do with the navy.
navy	a country's warships and sailors.
near	close to: not far away.

nearly	almost: not quite. We had **nearly** reached the top of the hill.
neat	clean and tidy.
necessary	needful: something that we must have or that must be done.
neck	the part of the body joining the head and shoulders.
necklace	a string of beads or jewels worn round the neck. The lady was wearing a diamond **necklace.**
need	to want badly.
needle	a thin piece of metal used for sewing.
neglect	not to do something which should be done.
negro	a man who has a black skin.
neigh	the sound made by a horse.
neighbour	a person who lives quite near.
neither	not one or the other.
nephew	a son of a brother or sister.
nervous	afraid: timid. She went **nervously** on to the stage.
nest	a bed where a bird lays its eggs.
nestle	to cuddle closely. The chickens **nestled** together.
net	string or cord woven to leave openings.

nettle	a wild plant which can sting us.
never	not ever: not at any time.
new	just made: never used.
news	telling or writing about something that has just happened.
newt	a small land or water animal like a small lizard.
next	1. touching: nearest. 2. following.
nib	the point of a pen.
nibble	to take tiny bites of food.
nice	pleasant: delicious.
nickname	a name given to us which is not our real name.
niece	the daughter of a brother or a sister.
nigh	1. close to. 2. nearly: almost.
night	the time of darkness.
nimble	quick and light on the feet.
nine	9. a number, one less than ten. John was **ninth** in the class.
nineteen	19. a number, ten and nine added together. I had **nineteen** sums correct.
ninety	90. a number, nine tens. The man scored **ninety** runs at cricket.
nip	to pinch or bite the skin.
no	1. none at all. 2. a word of refusal.

noble	1. splendid: remarkable. 2. brave.	**noun**	the name of something.
nobleman	a person of high rank.	**nourish**	to feed with food that will keep us healthy.
nobody	no one: a person of no importance.	**nourishment**	the right food to keep us healthy.
nod	to bend the head forward quickly.	**now**	at present: at this moment.
noise	din, clatter. The crowd at the game was **noisy**. The children ran away **noisily**.	**nowadays**	at this time: at present.
		nozzle	the open end of a tube or a spout.
		nudge	a slight push.
none	not any: not one.	**nuisance**	1. something which annoys us. 2. anything which hinders us and holds us up.
nonsense	stupid talk.		
noon	twelve o'clock mid-day.		
noose	a loop which can be made tighter by pulling.	**number**	1. a word or figure that tells how much. 2. a crowd: a quantity.
nor	and not.		
normal	usual: the same as the others.	**numerous**	plenty: a large number.
north	the direction opposite the sun at mid-day.	**nun**	a woman who lives a religious life in a convent.
nose	the part of the head with which we smell.	**nurse**	a person trained to help sick people or children.
nostril	an opening in the nose.	**nursery**	1. a room for the use of young children. 2. a place where young plants are grown from seed.
not	a word refusing to allow us to do something.		
notch	a tiny cut or dent.		
note	1. a short letter. 2. a sound in music. 3. a piece of paper money.	**nut**	1. the seed of a tree. 2. a piece of metal which screws on to a bolt.
nothing	not a single thing: none at all.	**nutmeg**	a spice used in cooking.
notice	1. to see something. 2. a paper telling us some news.	**nylon**	a material made from artificial threads.
nought	the figure 0: nothing.	**nymph**	a lovely girl or goddess in tales of long ago.

O

oak	a tree of very hard wood.
oar	a long flat wooden bar used to drive a rowing boat.
oasis	a fertile place where water is found in a desert.
oats	a corn crop.
obedience	when we obey somebody.
obey	to do as we are told. The boy was always **obedient.**
object	something that we can see or touch.
object	to grumble about. As there was an **objection,** he did not run in the race.
oblige	1. to do a favour to somebody. 2. to compel somebody to do something.
oblong	a four-sided figure longer than it is broad.
observe	to see: to look at.
obstacle	something which is in the way. We found the **obstacle** race most amusing.
obstruct	to block the way: to hinder. The broken-down lorry was an **obstruction** in the roadway.
obtain	to get.
obvious	easy to see or understand.
occasion	an event: a happening.
occupy	1. to live in. 2. to spend time in. A man's **occupation** is the work he does.
occur	to take place: to happen.
ocean	a large sea.
o'clock	the time shown by the clock.
odd	1. not even. 1, 3, 5, are **odd** numbers. 2. strange: unusual. It was **odd** that he broke his promise.
odour	a smell: a scent.
of	the top **of** the class. There were three **of** us.
off	from. The boy jumped **off** the wall.
offend	1. to make somebody unhappy: to displease. 2. to break the rules or the law.
offer	1. to say that we are ready to do something. 2. to hold a thing out for somebody to take.
office	a room for writing.
officer	the person who is in charge.
oft(en)	many times.
ogre	a fearful giant heard of in fairy tales.
oil	thin greasy fat used to make machinery work smoothly.
ointment	a healing grease used on cuts and bruises.

old	of great age. In history, we learn about **olden** times. The room was filled with **old-fashioned** things.
omit	to leave out.
omnibus	a bus: a motor coach.
once	1. one time. 2. in the past.
one	a single person or thing.
onion	a root vegetable which is often cooked before it is eaten.
only	by itself: single.
onward	on and on: forward.
open	not shut: not covered over.
operate	1. to act. 2. to perform an operation.
operation	an action by a doctor to make us better.
opposite	on the far side of: facing.
oral	spoken aloud.
orange	1. a round yellow fruit which is grown in hot lands. 2. a colour.
orbit	the path of one body round another in space.
orchard	a garden of fruit trees and bushes.
ordeal	a great trial or test.
order	1. form: method. 2. to say what must be done.
ordinary	what we expect: usual.
organ	1. a part of the body. 2. a musical instrument with keys arranged like a piano.
original	the first one: the earliest.
ornament	a decoration for the body or for a room.
orphan	a child whose father or mother or both are dead.
ostler	a servant who looks after horses.
ostrich	the largest of the birds. It has beautiful feathers but cannot fly.
other	different: not the same.
otherwise	in a different way.
otter	a land and water animal.
ought	You **ought** to go.
ounce	a measure of weight.
our(s)	belonging to us.
ourselves	we or us alone.
out	1. not in. We looked **outside** for him. 2. not burning.
outlaw	a person who has broken the law and is being looked for by the police.
oval	the shape of an egg.
oven	a special place for cooking and baking.
over	1. above. 2. done: finished.
overboard	over the side of a ship. The rope was thrown **overboard.**
overtake	to pass and leave behind.
owe	to be in debt: to have to pay.
owl	a large bird which calls at night by hooting.

own
1. belonging to me.
2. to have: to possess.
    We tried to find the **owner.**

ox
an animal like a cow.
The **oxen** were pulling the cart.

oyster
a shellfish used for food and in which pearls are occasionally found.

P

pace
1. a stride or step.
2. how quickly we walk.

pack
1. to put into a box or parcel.
    A large wooden **package** was put on the train.
2. a group of things such as playing cards.
    Mary bought a **packet** of crisps.
3. a group of animals of the same sort.

pad
1. several sheets of paper together such as a **writing pad.**
2. soft material such as cotton wool.

paddle
1. an oar for driving a boat or a canoe.
2. to walk in shallow water.

page
1. a leaf of a book.
2. a boy servant in a hotel.

pageant
a parade of history in costume.

pail
a bucket.

pain
hurt: suffering.
A bad tooth is often **painful.**

paint
liquid colour which is put on with a brush.
The **painter** climbed slowly up the ladder.

pair
two of anything such as a **pair** of socks.

palace
a large mansion often lived in by kings and queens.

pale
dull: with little colour.

palm
1. a tree which grows in hot lands.
2. the flat front of the hand.

pamper
to allow somebody to do as they please: to give in to.

pan
a metal can for cooking.

panda
a black and white animal like a small bear.

pane
a piece of glass for a window.

panel
a piece of material fitted into a frame or into a door.

panic
sudden alarm and fear which makes us behave in a stupid or thoughtless way.

pansy
a small flower like a violet but larger.

pant
to breathe quickly as though we are short of breath.

panther
a fierce, wild animal like a leopard.

pantomime
a nursery story performed on the stage.

pantry
a room or a large cupboard for storing food.
The two **pantries** were different in shape.

paper	material for writing, printing books, wrapping, and so on.
parable	a story with a meaning which will teach us a lesson.
parachute	cloth shaped like an umbrella for saving the lives of air travellers who have to jump out of aeroplanes.
parade	1. a marching display by people in uniform. 2. to march up and down.
paraffin	thin oil used in lamps and stoves.
paragraph	a small part of a story: several sentences grouped together.
parcel	things wrapped together into a bundle or a package.
pardon	forgiveness for a wrong we have done.
pare	to trim: to cut away: to peel.
parent	father or mother.
parish	a district looked after by a clergyman.
park	1. a piece of land for everybody to use, usually having grass, and flowers. 2. land on which cars may be left.
parliament	a group of people who make our laws.
parlour	the sitting-room of a house.
parrot	a bird which can talk and which has bright feathers.
parsley	a herb used in cooking.
parsnip	a pale root vegetable which we may eat.
parson	a minister: a clergyman.
part	1. a share. 2. to separate: to split up. We were upset as the time of **parting** drew near.
particle	a tiny piece.
particular	1. hard to please. 2. special and important.
partition	a screen or wall between two rooms.
partner	one who helps us in work or in play.
party	a group of people together. Christmas is a time for children's **parties.**
pass	1. to overtake: to leave behind. 2. to get through a test. 3. a gap in the mountains.
passage	1. a narrow way through. 2. a piece taken from a book or a story.
passenger	a person who travels in a train, bus, ship or car.
paste	a mixture which is put on to things to stick them together.
pastime	a hobby: interesting work done in our spare time.
pastry	baked flour and water used to make a pie or a tart.
pasture	grass-land for feeding animals.
pat	to touch gently with the hand.
patch	material used to repair a hole.

path	a place for walking.
patience	calmness when we are waiting.
patter	the sound made by:— 1. raindrops. 2. running feet.
pattern	1. a drawing or design. 2. a plan to follow.
pause	a short stop or wait.
pave	to place flat stones side by side to make a path. We should walk on the **pavement.**
paw	an animal's foot.
pay	to hand over money that we owe: wages. We made **payment** for what we had bought.
pea	a small seed which grows in a pod.
peace	1. when we are not at war. 2. quietness: stillness. The scene was **peaceful** as the sun sank below the hills.
peach	a soft juicy fruit which grows in hot lands.
peak	1. the top of a hill or a mountain. 2. the front of a cap.
peal	1. the sound of bells. 2. the sound of thunder.
pear	a juicy, pointed fruit.
pearl	a precious gem found in an oyster shell.

pebble	a smooth, rounded stone often found on the beach.
peck	to nibble at food.
peculiar	strange: unusual.
pedal	a bar or lever which we move with the feet to drive a machine.
pedestrian	a person who walks.
pedlar	one who sells small things which he carries from house to house.
peel	1. the outside skin of fruit or vegetables. 2. to take off the skin from fruit or vegetables.
peep	to glance at: to look at something with half-closed eyes.
peer	1. to look at closely. 2. a person of high rank.
peg	a small clip for hanging clothes.
pelt	1. an animal's skin and fur. 2. to throw things at something or someone.
pen	1. a tool which is used when writing with ink. 2. a part fenced in to keep animals together.
penalty	a punishment for breaking a rule or the law.
pencil	a writing tool made of wood with a black or coloured centre.
penetrate	to go into: to go through.
penguin	a sea-bird found in cold lands in the south and which cannot fly.

penny	a coin. A hundred new **pence** make one pound. The man said that he was quite **penniless.**
pension	money which is paid to us when we can no longer work.
people	men, women and children.
pepper	a powder which is used for flavouring.
perch	1. a rail on which a bird can rest. 2. a fresh-water fish.
perfect	with nothing wrong: absolutely correct.
perform	to act: to do. The acrobat gave a wonderful **performance.**
perfume	scent: a pleasing smell.
perhaps	maybe: possibly.
peril	much danger.
period	a length of time.
perish	to die: to wither away.
permit	to allow: to let somebody do something. We asked for **permission** to go into the field.
persist	to do something again and again: to refuse to stop.
person	a man, a woman or a child.
perspire	to sweat.
persuade	to talk to a person until he does as we wish.
pest	a person, animal or insect that causes trouble.
pester	to annoy somebody.
pet	an animal which we keep for pleasure.
petal	the brightly-coloured leaf of a flower.
petrol	motor spirit: the liquid that drives the engine of a motor-car.
pew	a seat or bench in a church.
pheasant	a wild bird with a long tail and beautiful feathers.
phone	a shortened way of writing the word 'telephone'.
photograph	a picture taken using a camera.
phrase	a few words which are part of a sentence.
piano	a musical instrument played by pressing the keys.
pick	1. to gather. We went to **pick** flowers. 2. to choose. 3. a pointed metal tool. The man used a **pick** to make a hole in the road.
pickle	vegetables kept in salt or in vinegar.
picnic	a meal in the open air.
picture	a drawing, a painting or a photograph.
pie	fruit or meat cooked in a crust of pastry.
piece	a scrap: a part.
pier	a landing-stage for ships built out into the sea.
pierce	to stab: to make a hole in something.
pig	a four-legged animal kept for making bacon and pork.

pigeon	a bird which can find its way home.
pile	a large heap.
pilgrim	a person who travels to visit a holy place.
pill	a tiny ball of medicine.
pillar	an upright post which is often used to hold up a part of a building.
pillow	the cushion used on a bed.
pilot	a man who steers a boat or an aeroplane.
pin	a thin sharp piece of pointed metal which is used for **pinning** things together.
pinafore	a full length apron.
pincers	a tool with jaws which grip when closed.
pinch	to nip tightly with the fingers.
pine	1. to long for something or somebody very much. 2. a tall tree on which cones grow.
pink	a pale red colour.
pint	a measure of liquids.
pipe	1. a tube which is often made of metal or rubber. 2. a bowl with a stem for smoking tobacco. 3. a musical instrument.

pirate	a sea robber.
pistol	a short gun: a revolver.
pit	a hole in or under the ground.
pitch	1. a length of ground for playing games. 2. tar.
pitcher	a large water pot usually made of baked clay.
pity	when we feel sorry for somebody. The shipwrecked sailors were a **pitiful** sight.
place	a position: a town.
plague	a terrible disease which spreads very quickly.
plaice	a flat sea fish.
plain	1. ordinary: simple. 2. a flat piece of land.
plait	(say 'plat') to weave by going under and over threads.
plan	1. a drawing of something. 2. to arrange.
plane	1. an aeroplane. 2. a tool for smoothing wood.
planet	a heavenly body that moves round the sun.
plank	a thick, flat piece of wood.
plant	1. something which grows from roots in the ground. 2. to put seeds into soil so that they may grow. The men worked on a cotton **plantation.** The rubber **plant**er rode round the estate.

F

plaster	1. a smooth covering for walls. 2. a healing paste put on to a wound.	**plug**	a stopper for a bath or a bowl.
plate	a flat dish from which we eat our food.	**plum**	a stony fruit which grows on trees.
platform	a raised place at a railway station or in a hall.	**plumber**	a man who fits and repairs water and gas pipes.
play	1. a story which is acted. 2. to join in a game. 3. to make sounds on a musical instrument.	**plump**	rather fat.
		plunder	to rob: to steal from somebody using force.
plead	to ask sincerely: to beg.	**plunge**	to dive in.
pleasant	delightful: pleasing.	**plural**	more than one.
please	to make somebody happy.	**plus**	added to: the sign +.
pleasure	happiness: joy.	**poach**	1. to cook an egg in water. 2. to trap and steal animals on private ground.
pleat	a fold which is pressed into clothes.	**pocket**	a bag made in our clothes.
plenty	more than enough. The boat brought in a **plentiful** supply of fish.	**pod**	a seed case on a plant.
		poem	words written in verses.
pliers	a tool which will grip when closed: small pincers.	**poet**	a person who writes poems. We have **poetry** lessons at school.
plimsoll	a rubber-soled shoe used in many games.	**point**	1. the sharp end. 2. to show with a finger.
plot	1. the story of a play. 2. a piece of ground. 3. a plan to be carried out.	**poison**	a substance which could kill us or make us very ill. We were warned that the berries were **poisonous.**
plough	a machine for breaking up the soil.	**poke**	to stab with a stick or a rod. The fire was made brighter by using a **poker.**
pluck	1. bravery. 2. to take the feathers from a dead bird. 3. to gather flowers.	**polar**	connected with the north and south poles.
		pole	a thick bar or stick.

police	people who make sure that the law is kept.
polish	to make smooth and bright. The car was beautifully **polished.**
polite	well-mannered: well-be-haved. Children should show **politeness** to older people.
poll	to vote at an election.
pollen	fine yellow dust found in flowers.
pomegranate	a fruit grown in hot countries.
pond	a small lake.
ponder	to think about something carefully.
pony	a small horse. The **ponies** were grazing in the fields.
poodle	a small dog kept as a pet.
pool	a small patch of water.
poor	1. not rich: not having much money. 2. not very good.
pop	a sudden noise.
poplar	a tree which has a rough bark and which grows very quickly.
poppy	a plant which has brightly-coloured flowers.
popular	well liked by other people.
population	people who live in a certain country or town.
porch	a shelter over an outside door of a building.
pores	tiny holes in the skin.

pork	meat from a pig made ready to cook and eat.
porpoise	a sea animal rather like a small whale.
port	1. a place where ships land their cargo. 2. a red wine.
portable	able to be carried about. We were listening to a **portable** wireless set.
porter	a man who carries parcels and luggage at a station or a hotel.
portion	a part or a share of something.
portrait	a drawing, a painting or a photograph of a person.
position	the place for something or somebody.
positive	certain: quite sure.
possess	to have: to own. The boy took **possession** of the ball he had been given.
possible	able to be done: likely to take place. We knew that it could **possibly** happen.
post	1. a pole fixed in the ground. 2. the way we send and receive letters. The **postman** brought the letters. Each envelope had a **postage** stamp. One envelope contained a **postal** order.
poster	a large notice for people to read.

potato — a root vegetable which we eat.
The **potatoes** were boiling in a pan.

pottery — 1. articles such as cups, which are made of baked clay.
2. the place where these things are made.

pound — 1. a measure of weight.
2. an amount of money equal to a hundred new pence.
3. to thump.

pour — 1. to flow away.
2. to rain heavily.

powder — dust made by crushing a hard substance.

power — strength.
The boat was towed by a **powerful** tug.

practice — 1. the doing of a thing again and again.
2. a habit.
Practice makes us perfect.

practise — to do a thing again and again.
The girl had to **practise** to play the piano so well.

prairie — large stretches of grassland.

praise — to speak well of a person.

pram — a small carriage for a baby: a perambulator.

prance — to move about jerkily on the back legs.

prawn — a small shell fish.

pray — 1. to ask very sincerely.
2. to speak to God.
The church service opened with a **prayer**.

preach — 1. to tell somebody what to do.
2. to give a sermon.
The **preacher** went into the pulpit.

precious — very valuable.

precipice — a steep and dangerous cliff.

prefect — a boy or girl who helps to keep order in a school.

prefer — to like most: to like one person or thing more than the others.

prepare — to make ready.
We were making **preparations** for the trip.

present — 1. a gift.
2. to be there.
We were shown into the **presence** of the queen.

present — to hand over to.
He was **presented** with his prize.

presently — in a short time: shortly: soon.

preserve — to keep safely out of harm and danger.

president — the chief man of a country or of a group of men.

press — 1. to push hard.
2. to crush something.
3. a machine for printing.

pretend — to act as though we are somebody or something else.

pretty — attractive: delightful to see.

prevent — to stop something from taking place.

previous	before.	**prize**	a reward which is given to us when we win.
prey	something that is being hunted.	**probable**	likely to take place.
price	how much we must pay to buy something: the cost.	**probably**	likely to be.
		problem	a difficult thing to decide.
priceless	almost too costly to buy. The queen was wearing **priceless** jewels.	**proceed**	to go forward: to carry on after stopping.
prick	to stab with something pointed.	**procession**	an orderly march.
		prod	to poke: to stab roughly.
prickle	a thorn or thistle. Some plants have **prickly** stems.	**produce**	1. to bring out: to show. 2. to make.
pride	when we think that we have been very clever: conceit.	**produce**	something that has been made or grown.
priest	a clergyman: a parson.	**profit**	gain: money that we make when we sell something for more than we paid for it.
primary	first: earliest.		
primrose	a yellow flower.	**progress**	a move forward.
prince	a man or boy of royal birth.	**progress**	to go onwards: to advance.
princess	a woman or girl of royal birth.	**promenade**	a special place for walking at the seaside.
principal	most important: chief: head.	**promise**	to say what we will do.
principle	a rule which we must keep.	**prompt**	in good time: at the right time. The concert began **promptly**.
print	1. single letters. 2. to press letters on to paper by a machine. The **printer** was preparing the machine.		
		prong	the sharp spike of a fork.
		pronoun	a word used in place of a noun.
prior	1. sooner: earlier. 2. one of the chief men in a monastery.	**pronounce**	to speak clearly.
		proof	something that shows what is the truth.
prison	a place where criminals are kept. The **prisoner** was taken to be tried.	**prop**	to hold up something to prevent it from falling.
		propeller	blades which drive an aeroplane or a ship.
private	not public: about ourselves alone.	**proper**	correct: right.
privet	a shrub used to make hedges.	**property**	something owned.

prophet	a man who can say what is going to happen.
propose	to suggest: to offer.
prosecute	to summon someone in a police court.
prosper	to do well: to succeed.
protect	to look after: to defend. The wall had been built for **protection**.
protest	to object to: to speak against.
proud	when we are very pleased with ourselves. The winner walked forward **proudly**.
prove	to show that something is true.
proverb	a wise saying with a special meaning.
provide	to supply: to give something that is needed.
prowl	to move quietly when we are hunting for something.
pry	to ask about things which are not our business.
psalm	a bible poem or song.
public	well-known: for everybody to use.
pudding	a soft, cooked food.
puddle	a small pool of dirty water.
puff	1. a short blast of breath or smoke. 2. a pad for powdering the skin.
pull	to drag something towards us.
pullet	a young hen, usually less than a year old.

pulp	squashed fruit or vegetables.
pulpit	a raised platform from which a sermon is preached.
pulse	the beating of the heart.
pump	an instrument for blowing up tyres or for lifting water.
punch	to hit with the fist.
punctual	at the time arranged: not late.
punctuation	full stops, commas and other such marks used in writing.
puncture	a small hole often made by something pointed.
punish	to make a guilty person suffer for what he has done. The boy's spending money was stopped as a **punishment**.
pupil	1. a scholar: a learner. 2. the dark centre part of the eye.
puppet	a doll which can be made to move by pulling strings or by placing on the hand like a glove.
puppy	a young dog.
purchase	to buy: to pay money for something.
pure	clean and spotless. The bottle was washed in boiling water to **purify** it.
purple	a colour made by mixing red and blue.
purpose	what we intend to do.
purposely	knowing quite well what we were doing.

purr	the noise made by a cat when it is pleased.
purse	a small bag used for holding money.
pursue	to chase after. The policeman set off in **pursuit** of the thief.
push	to press against something to try to move it.
put	to place in position.
putty	a soft mixture used to hold glass in a frame.
puzzle	a problem: a difficulty.
pyjamas	the jacket and trousers in which we sleep.
pylon	a metal tower used to hold up electric cables.
pyramid	a building which is square at the bottom and pointed at the top.
python	a dangerous snake.

Q

quack	the noise made by ducks.
quaint	unusual: strange: odd.
quake	to shake: to tremble. The town was shaken by a violent **earthquake.**
quality	the goodness of a thing.
quantity	the amount: the number.
quarrel	to disagree angrily with someone: to argue. She was a **quarrelsome** girl.
quarry	1. a place where stone is dug from the earth. 2. an animal that is being hunted.
quart	a measure of liquids.
quarter	one of four equal parts: a fourth part of something.
quay	(say 'key') a landing-stage for ships.
queen	1. the wife of a king. 2. a lady ruler.
queer	peculiar: strange. The dog was behaving **queerly.**
quell	to put down a disturbance: to put a stop to.
quench	1. to end a thirst. 2. to put out a fire.
query	a question.
question	something that needs to be answered: an enquiry.
queue	(say 'Q') a line of waiting people.
quick	fast: at great speed: swift. Rescue workers were **quickly** on the scene.
quickness	speed: hurry.
quiet	peaceful: not noisy. We entered the room **quietly.** There must be **quietness** at an examination.
quill	1. a long feather. 2. a pen made from such a feather.
quilt	a covering for a bed.
quit	to leave: to go away.
quite	perfectly: fully: completely.

quiver	1. to tremble. 2. a holder for arrows.
quiz	a question or a number of questions to be answered: a test.
quote	to repeat exactly what somebody has spoken or written.

R

rabbit	a small furry animal which lives in holes in the ground.
race	1. a test of speed. 2. people of the same kind or colour.
rack	a frame or bar for holding things.
racket	1. a bat used in tennis. 2. a great noise.
radar	a method of helping to guide ships and aeroplanes by using electricity.
radiator	1. an instrument which sends out heat. 2. the front part of the engine of a motor-car.
radio	sounds sent from one place to another with no wires between the places.
radish	a small, reddish, root vegetable used in salads.
raffia	coloured straw made from large leaves.
raffle	a game of chance to win a prize.
raft	a wooden platform made to float on water.
rafter	a beam which holds up the slates in a roof.

rag	a piece of waste cloth. The tramp was dressed in **ragged** clothing.
rage	great anger: violent temper.
raid	a sudden attack which was not expected. The **raiders** were finally driven off.
rail	a wooden or a metal bar.
railway	the engines, carriages, lines and all the other things connected with trains.
raiment	clothing: garments.
rain	drops of water falling from the clouds. A perfect **rainbow** appeared in the sky.
raise	to lift up: to make higher.
raisins	dried grapes often used in cakes and puddings.
rake	a garden tool fitted with spikes.
rally	1. to gather people together after they have been separated. 2. to begin to get better after being very ill.
ram	1. a male sheep. 2. to smash into something.
ramble	1. a country walk. 2. to wander about. 3. to talk foolishly and without thinking.
ranch	a large sheep or cattle farm.
random	by chance: anyhow.
range	1. a kitchen stove. 2. a distance that a gun can shoot.

rank	1. a line or a row. 2. the class or title of a person.
ransom	a sum of money to buy a prisoner's freedom.
rap	a sharp tap or blow.
rapid	fast: quick. The sky cleared **rapidly.**
rare	scarce: not often seen.
rarely	hardly ever. I **rarely** travel by train.
rascal	a villain: a bad person.
rash	1. thoughtless: hasty. 2. a large number of spots on the skin.
raspberry	red, juicy berries.
rat	a fierce animal like a large mouse.
rate	1. the speed at which something goes. 2. the price that has been fixed.
rather	more willingly: sooner.
ration	a share of something when there is not a large amount to share.
rattle	the noise of things being shaken together.
rave	to shout and scream: to talk wildly.
raven	a large black bird.
ravenous	very hungry indeed: famished.
ravine	a deep gorge: a cleft.

raw	1. not cooked: fresh. I ate a **raw** plum. 2. cold: chilly: bleak. In January, the weather is often **raw.**
ray	a shaft or a beam of light.
razor	a sharp tool for shaving.
reach	1. to stretch and touch. 2. to arrive at a certain place.
read	to understand the meaning of printed words. John became an excellent **reader.**
ready	prepared: willing.
readily	gladly: willingly. He **readily** agreed to do as we wished.
real	actual: true: not false. We could not believe that it was **really** true.
realize	to understand the truth of what we have been told.
realm	a kingdom: the land which is ruled by one person.
reap	to gather in: to collect a crop.
rear	1. the back part. 2. to rise into the air.
reason	the cause: the explanation.
reasonable	right: sensible.
rebel	to rise against the leader. The king's troops put down the **rebellion.**
rebel	one who rises against the leader.

rebound	to bounce back.
rebuke	to find fault with and to check somebody.
recall	1. to call somebody back. 2. to remember.
receipt	a paper stating that something has been received.
receive	to take: to accept something that is given or sent.
recent	new: just happened. They had **recently** moved.
recipe	a list of instructions telling us how to cook or to bake a certain thing.
recite	to say aloud and from memory.
reckon	to add up: to count.
recognise	to know something or somebody again.
record	1. a gramophone disc. His **record-player** was a birthday present. 2. something that has not been beaten.
record	1. to write down. 2. to make a speech or music on a gramophone disc.
recover	1. to get a thing back. 2. to get better after an illness.
re-cover	to put on a new cover.
recreation	games played and hobbies done in our spare time.
rectangle	an oblong. A book back or a sheet of paper is usually shaped like a **rectangle.**
red	a colour: the colour of blood.

reduce	to bring down the cost of something: to make something less.
reef	rocks just below the level of the sea.
reel	1. a bobbin of cotton. 2. a quick dance. 3. to stagger about.
refer	to talk about: to remind us about: to recall. An atlas is a **reference** book.
referee	the person who makes sure that a game is fairly played: an umpire.
reflect	to show or to shine back. The dog could see its **reflection** in the water.
refresh	to make us feel less tired.
refreshment	food and drink which refresh us.
refuge	a place of safety.
refuse	to decline: to say 'No'. We were surprised at his **refusal** to play.
refuse	rubbish such as things thrown into a dustbin.
regard	to look at: to view.
regiment	a large band of soldiers.
region	a part of the world or of a country: a district.
register	a list of names and addresses kept for a special reason.
regret	to be very sorry about.
regular	constant: steady: usual. We go to the swimming-baths **regularly.**

reign	1. the length of time a ruler is on the throne. 2. to rule as a king or queen.
reins	the straps used to control and guide a horse.
reindeer	an animal which has long horns and which lives in the cold, northern lands.
reject	to refuse to take something: to throw away.
rejoice	to be very glad about something.
relation **relative**	someone in the same family such as father, mother, son, aunt and so on.
relay	1. to send a message from one place to another. 2. a team race.
release	to allow to go free.
reliable	able to be trusted.
relic	a thing left from past times, often something holy.
relief	1. help for people in trouble. 2. when we hear good news after being in trouble or difficulty.
religion	belief in God: the way a person worships. They were a **religious** people.
rely	to depend on: to count on. We knew from what he had done that he was a **reliable** man.

remain	to stay behind. In some division sums there is a **remainder**.
remark	to speak about: to say something about.
remarkable	unusual: wonderful.
remedy	a cure.
remember	to recall: to call to mind.
remind	to make somebody remember.
remove	1. to take away. 2. to move from one place to another. The men were loading the **removal** van.
rent	1. the money we pay for the use of a house. 2. a tear in cloth.
repair	to mend: to put right.
repeat	to say or to do again.
repent	to be very sorry about some wrong that we have done.
reply	to answer either by speaking or by writing.
report	1. to say or write about what has taken place. 2. a loud noise such as that made by firing a gun.
reptile	an animal with no legs like a snake, or with tiny legs like a lizard.
request	to ask for something to be done.

require	to need: to want.
rescue	to save: to take out of danger.
reserve	1. to keep something until it is needed. 2. something spare or extra.
reservoir	a large lake of water which has been specially made to supply a town or city.
reside	to dwell: to live.
respect	to admire: to look up to. She seemed to be a **respectable** old lady.
rest	1. the others: the remainder. 2. to be quiet: not to work.
restaurant	a café: a place for eating.
restore	1. to give back. 2. to clean and repair something.
result	the happening at the end: the conclusion.
retire	1. to withdraw: to leave and go away. 2. to go to bed. 3. to stop working because of age or illness.
retreat	to go back: to retire.
return	1. to come back. 2. to give back.
reveal	to show: to make something known either by speaking or by writing.
revenge	punishment for a wrong deed: to 'get our own back'.
reverse	1. to go backwards. 2. to go in the opposite direction.
revise	to read over what we have written and correct and improve it.
revolt	to mutiny: to turn against the leader.
revolution	1. a mutiny: a revolt. 2. the turning round of a wheel.
revolver	a small gun for shooting bullets: a pistol.
reward	payment for a brave or a good deed.
rhinoceros	a large animal with horns, found in Africa.
rhubarb	a garden plant with juicy stalks which can be eaten.
rhyme	word endings which sound alike. The children were learning a nursery **rhyme**.
rhythm	the steady beat or time of poetry or music.
rib	a bone across the chest.
ribbon	a narrow band of material.
rice	a food grown in Eastern lands.
rid	to be free of.
riddle	1. a puzzle in words. 2. a tool used by gardeners for sifting dirt and stones.
ride	to be moved in a carriage or on an animal. The children were **riding** their horses.
ridicule	to make fun of somebody. We were asked to do a **ridiculous** thing.
rifle	a long-barrelled gun.
right	1. correct: not wrong. 2. good: true. 3. the opposite to the left.

rim	the edge of such things as bowls or wheels.
rind	the hard edge: the crust.
ring	1. a round piece of metal. 2. a circle. 3. the sound made by a bell.
rink	a place made specially for skating.
rinse	to wash with clean water.
riot	a disturbance caused by people quarrelling violently.
rip	a tear: a split.
ripe	ready for eating because it is fully grown.
ripple	a tiny wave on water.
rise	1. to go higher. 2. to get up.
risk	a danger: a difficulty. To climb the rock was known to be **risky.**
rival	a person who tries to equal or do better than another person.
river	a large stream.
road	a wide track on which vehicles move.
roam	to wander about.
roar	a loud, deep sound: the noise made by a lion or by thunder.
roast	to cook in fat before a fire or in an oven.

rob	to steal: to take something that does not belong to us. Nobody saw the car used in the **robbery.**
robe	a long, loose gown.
robin	a small, friendly, red-breasted bird.
rock	1. large pieces of stone. The boat was wrecked on the **rocky** shore. The lady was arranging plants on the **rockery.** 2. to move from side to side. 3. a minty sweet.
rocket	something driven into the air by gas or an explosion.
rod	a thin bar of wood or metal.
rogue	a scoundrel: a person that we cannot trust.
roll	1. to turn over and over. A **roller** was used on the cricket pitch. 2. a tube of anything such as a **roll** of wall-paper. 3. the sound made by drums.
roof	1. the covering of a building. 2. the top part of the inside of the mouth.
rook	a black bird of the crow family. The noise from the **rookery** was deafening.
room	1. a part of a house. 2. a space in which things may be kept.

roost	a place for fowls to rest in.	**rubber**	1. the name of a tree grown in hot lands. 2. **rubber** is made from the sap of the **rubber** tree.
root	the part of a plant which is in the soil.		
rope	a thick cord.	**rubbish**	1. waste things that are of no use. 2. nonsense.
rose	a sweet-smelling flower often found in hedges and in gardens.	**ruby**	a precious red stone.
rosy	pink in colour.	**rudder**	a piece of wood or metal fixed at the back to steer a boat or an aeroplane.
rot	to decay: to go bad and perish. The dead branch of the tree was **rotten.**	**rude**	not polite: rough.
		ruffian	a rough, cruel person.
		ruffle	to disturb: to upset.
rouge	red powder or paint used for colouring the lips or face.	**rug**	1. a small carpet: a mat. 2. a wrap or cover used when travelling.
rough	1. not smooth: coarse. 2. wild and stormy.	**ruin**	1. a building which is falling down. 2. to wreck: to spoil something.
round	the same shape as a ball or ring. We each had a turn on the **roundabout.**	**rule**	1. a law that we must follow. 2. a measuring rod or tape. 3. to govern.
rounders	a game played by two sides with bat and ball.	**ruler**	1. a governor. 2. a measuring rod often used for drawing straight lines.
rouse	to wake up: to stir up.		
route	the way or road to go.	**rumble**	a deep roll of sound like the sound of thunder.
row (like 'low')	1. to drive a boat with oars. 2. a line of people or things.	**rumour**	gossip which may or may not be true.
row (like 'now')	a noisy quarrel.	**run**	to move very quickly on foot. He was the only **runner** to finish the race.
royal	connected with kings and queens.	**rung**	a step on a ladder.
rub	to move one thing against another many times.	**rush**	to move very quickly: to dash forward.

rust	a brown coating often found on damp iron and steel. The nails were no use because they were **rusty.**
rustle	a gentle, rubbing sound.
rye	a corn which is made into bread in some countries.

S

sabbath	the day for the worship of God.
sack	1. a large, rough, cloth bag. 2. to stop a person working.
sacred	holy: to do with the worship of God.
sacrifice	1. a gift to God. 2. when we give up something that we like very much.
sad	unhappy: distressed. The news of his illness filled us with **sadness.**
saddle	a leather seat for the rider of an animal or a cycle.
safe	1. a strong steel box. 2. out of danger. The firemen guided us to **safety.**
sag	to droop in the middle.
sage	1. a wise person. 2. a herb used in cooking.
sail	1. a large sheet on a boat to catch the wind and drive the boat along. 2. to ride in a boat. The **sailor** went to sea.
saint	a holy person.

sake	'for my **sake**' means 'to please me'.
salad	uncooked vegetables or fruit mixed together and made ready to eat.
salary	a wage which is usually paid each month.
sale	when things are sold.
salmon	a large fish with pink flesh which we may eat.
saloon	a large room or hall for the public to use.
salt	a mineral used for flavouring food. Sea water tastes **salty.**
salute	to greet by raising the hand to the forehead: to make very welcome.
same	not different: like.
sample	1. a pattern: a small piece to show what something is like. 2. to test.
sand	powdered rock often found at the seaside. We saw a **sandy** beach in the distance.
sandal	an open-topped shoe fastened with straps or cords.
sandwich	two pieces of bread with various foods between them.
sane	in one's right mind: normal: sensible.
sap	the liquid in the stems of plants and trees.

sapling	a young tree.
sardine	a small sea fish used as a food and often bought in small tins.
sash	1. a cord or ribbon. 2. a window-frame.
satchel	a child's school bag.
satin	a smooth, shiny, silky material used for ladies' clothes.
satisfy	to make others content and happy. To see them so healthy gave us great **satisfaction**. We were **satisfied**.
satellite	a natural or man-made body moving in space round a planet. The moon is a **satellite** of the earth. Television pictures from Australia come to us by **satellite**.
sauce	a liquid for flavouring food.
saucepan	a metal container which has a handle and is used for cooking.
saucer	a small flat dish on which we place a cup.
sausage	meat and bread mixed together in a skin.
savage	1. a wild human being. 2. fierce: angry.
save	1. to bring out of danger. 2. to store: to keep.
saw	a metal cutting-tool with sharp pointed teeth.
say	to speak.
scab	a covering which forms over a wound.
scabbard	a sheath for a sword or dagger.
scaffold	1. a framework on which builders work. 2. a platform used when people are hanged.
scald	to burn with hot liquid.
scale	1. a weighing-machine. 2. a ladder of musical notes. 3. to climb up to a height.
scalp	the skin and hair on the top of the head.
scamp	a person who is always in mischief.
scamper	to run quickly and lightly. The mouse **scampered** across the floor.
scandal	gossip and untrue tales about other people. We refused to do such a **scandalous** thing.
scar	a mark which has been left on the skin by a wound.
scarce	not common: rare.
scarcely	hardly: barely. The noise was so great that we could **scarcely** hear what was said.
scare	to frighten.
scarf	a square or length of cloth used as a covering for the neck and shoulders.
scarlet	bright red in colour.
scatter	to sprinkle things about.
scene	1. a view. 2. a part of a play. 3. the place where something happened.

scent	1. a smell: a perfume. 2. the trail of an animal.
scholar	1. a child at school. 2. a clever person.
school	1. a place where people, usually children, are taught. 2. a shoal of fish swimming together.
science	learning about nature and how things are made. The **scientist** was looking through a microscope.
scissors	a cutting tool with two blades fastened together.
scoff	to make fun of: to mock.
scoop	1. a shovel shaped like a bowl. 2. to dig with the hands.
scorch	to singe: to make something brown by burning it slightly.
score	1. a number, twenty. 2. to count or make points, runs or goals at games.
scorn	to think that something or somebody is of no value.
scoundrel	a villain: a bad man.
scout	1. a man sent to spy on the enemy. 2. a Boy Scout.
scowl	to frown: to give an angry look.
scramble	to move on hands and feet: to crawl.
scrap	1. a tiny piece. 2. rubbish thrown away.
scrape	1. a difficulty. 2. to rub and clean with a hard tool.
scratch	to mark with something sharp or pointed.
scrawl	to write badly: to scribble.
scream	a high-sounding shout or cry.
screech	a high-pitched noise like the noise made by an owl.
screen	1. a movable partition. 2. a sheet on which pictures are shown at a cinema.
screw	1. a nail with grooves round it. 2. a ship's propeller.
scribble	writing which is so poor that it cannot be read easily.
scribe	a writer.
scripture	the books of the Bible.
scroll	a rolled sheet of writing or drawing done in olden days.
scrub	1. to wash with water and a brush. 2. rough shrubs.
scuffle	a struggle or fight with much pushing.
scullery	a place where dishes are washed.
sculptor	a man who makes statues from wood or stone.
scuttle	1. a bucket in which coal is kept. 2. to run away quickly. 3. to sink a ship purposely by making holes in it.
scythe	a long blade which is used for cutting grass and which is fitted with a handle.

G

sea	salt water in the oceans. The rocks were covered with **seaweed**. The **seaman** wore a blue jersey.	**seem**	to appear to be: to look the same as.
seal	1. a sea animal that can live on land. 2. to stick and fasten an envelope. 3. wax with a special design or picture stamped on it.	**seer**	a person who can tell what is going to happen in the future: a prophet.

sea salt water in the oceans.
The rocks were covered with **seaweed**.
The **seaman** wore a blue jersey.

seal 1. a sea animal that can live on land.
2. to stick and fasten an envelope.
3. wax with a special design or picture stamped on it.

seam 1. a line where cloth is joined.
2. a layer of coal under the ground.

search to look for: to seek.

season 1. the time of the year such as spring, summer, autumn, winter.
2. to add something to food to make it taste better.

seat a place to sit.

second 1. next after the first.
The boy was attending a **secondary** school.
2. sixty **seconds** make a minute.
3. a man who helps a boxer at a boxing match.

secret something known only to a few people.

section a part or fraction of something.

secure firm: safe.

see what we are able to do with our eyes: to behold.

seed a tiny grain from which a plant grows.
A small plant may be called a **seedling**.

seek to search for: to look for.

seem to appear to be: to look the same as.

seer a person who can tell what is going to happen in the future: a prophet.

seesaw a rocking bar on which children sit.

seize to take hold of roughly: to grab.

seldom not often: rarely.

select to choose: to pick out.
In the shop was a good **selection** of flowers.

self one's own person such as oneself.

selfish thinking only about oneself.

sell to part with something for money.

semi placed in front of a word means 'half'. Therefore **semicircle** means 'half a circle'. **Semi-conscious** means 'half conscious'.

send to cause something to go: to dispatch.

senior older than others.

sense 1. the ability to act in a proper and understanding way.
His **sensible** action helped us out of a difficulty.
2. the power to be able to see, hear, smell, taste or touch.

sentence 1. a number of words together making sense.
2. a punishment given by a judge after a trial.

sentry a soldier on guard at a door or gate.

separate	to divide one thing from another thing.
septic	poisoned.
serial	a story told in parts or sections.
serious	1. of great importance. 2. dangerous. We were sorry to hear that he was **seriously** ill.
sermon	a message preached in a church or a chapel.
serpent	a snake: an animal without legs.

serve	1. to work for somebody.
	    The man had given excellent **service.**
	    She was a **servant** at the large house.
	2. to give out food.

serviette	a square of cloth or paper to keep us clean when we are eating.
set	1. to place things in order. 2. a whole group of things together. 3. a wireless or television receiver.
settee	a couch: a sofa: a seat for two or more people.
settle	1. to sink to the bottom. 2. to become still: to become calm. The quarrel ended in a peaceful **settlement.**
seven	7. a number, six and one added together.
seventeen	17. a number, seven and ten added together.
seventy	70. a number, seven tens.
sever	to cut off: to break off.

several	a number: a quantity.

severe	1. hard: strict.
	    Parents are **severe** to us if we do not speak the truth.
	2. very keen.
	    A **severe** frost froze the lake.

sew	to fasten with stitches: to use a needle and cotton.
shabby	1. almost worn out. 2. unkind and unjust.
shade	1. the sort of colour, either light or dark. 2. hidden from the sun or from the light and heat. We ate our meal in the **shadow** of the trees.
shaft	1. a piece of wood such as a handle or an arrow. 2. the entrance to a mine.
shake	to shiver: to tremble. We felt **shaky** after our narrow escape.
shallow	not deep.
sham	to pretend: to imitate something falsely.
shame	a feeling of sorrow because we have done wrong.
shampoo	a special soap for washing the hair.
shape	the form or appearance of anything.
share	1. the part given to each person. 2. to divide into parts.
shark	a large sea fish which will often attack people in the sea.

sharp	1. pointed: able to cut, stab or prick. 2. quick: fast. 3. intelligent.
shave	1. to remove hair by using a razor. 2. a narrow escape from danger or accident.
shawl	a covering for the head and shoulders often worn by women.
sheaf	a bundle of things tied together. The **sheaves** of corn were left in the field.
shear	to cut something off, using large scissors.
shears	large scissors used for cutting hedges or the wool from sheep.
sheath	1. a close-fitting cover. 2. a special cover for a sword.
shed	1. a hut, often made of wood. 2. to let fall. Many trees **shed** their leaves in autumn.
sheep	an animal reared for its wool and for its meat.
sheet	1. a large piece of cloth often used on a bed. 2. a thin, flat piece of glass or metal. 3. a stretch of water.
shelf	a ledge on which to store things. The **shelves** in the shop were filled with toys.
shell	1. a bony covering for a fish or a snail. 2. a large bullet.
shelter	a place where we are safe or where we are covered.
shepherd	a man who looks after sheep.
sheriff	the chief law officer of a district.
shield	1. something that protects us. 2. a plate of metal which knights held in front of themselves to protect them in battle.
shift	1. to take something from one place and put it in another place. 2. a number of men working together.
shin	the front of the leg between the knee and the ankle.
shine	1. to gleam. 2. to give out a light.
shingle	small stones on the seashore: pebbles.
ship	a sea-going boat. The lifeboat sailed to the scene of the **shipwreck**.
shirk	to dodge work: not to do something that we should do.
shirt	a cotton garment worn by men and boys.
shiver	to tremble because of cold or fear.
shoal	1. a batch of fish of the same sort swimming together. 2. a shallow place in the sea caused by a sand bank.

shock	1. a sudden violent surprise. 2. to be disgusted at something.
shoddy	badly made.
shoe	footwear worn below the ankles.
shoot	1. to fire a bullet or to send an arrow. 2. a young growth on a plant. 3. to move very quickly.
shop	a place where things are sold.
shore	where land and water meet at the beach or beside a lake.
short	1. not long: of small length. Mother used scissors to **shorten** the dress. 2. not enough. In a desert, there is a **shortage** of water.
shortly	soon. We expect to see them **shortly.**
shot	the sending of a bullet from a gun.
shoulder	the place where the arm joins the body.
shout	to speak in a loud voice.
shovel	a wide, flat spade used to scoop up things.
show	1. where special things are able to be seen: a **flower show.** 2. to allow to see. Please **show** me your presents.
shower	when rain falls lightly.
shred	a tiny piece. There was not a **shred** of truth in what he said.
shriek	a high-pitched scream of pain, surprise or laughter.
shrimp	a small shellfish found in sandy places.
shrink	1. to become smaller. 2. to draw back because of shyness or fear.
shrub	a small, bushy tree.
shudder	to shake with horror: to tremble.
shunt	to move railway trucks and carriages from one track to another.
shy	timid: afraid to speak.
sick	ill: unwell. The roll of the boat gave us a **sickly** feeling. The doctor told us how to avoid sea **sickness.**
side	1. a team at games. 2. one face of an object.
sideways	towards one side. We turned **sideways.**
siege	when a building or a town is surrounded so that no help or food can reach it.
sift	to separate: to examine.
sigh	a low moan caused by tiredness or sadness.
sight	1. when we are able to see. 2. something that we see.
sign	1. a movement or message which has a meaning for us. 2. to write one's name. Father wrote his **signature** on the paper.

signal	a sign or message telling us what to do.
	The **signal** showed the driver whether to go or stop.
silence	quietness: stillness.
	We remained **silent** until he had finished.
silk	smooth, shiny material often used for ladies' clothes.
silly	foolish: stupid.
silver	a costly, white metal used in the making of forks, spoons, ornaments and coins.
similar	like: almost the same as something else.
simple	1. easy: a **simple** sum.
	The exercise was done quite **simply**.
	2. plain: a **simple** dress.
sin	evil: wrongdoing.
since	1. from that time until now.
	2. because: as.
sincere	true: reliable.
	We often finish a letter by writing, 'Yours **sincerely**'.
sing	to make tunes with the voice.
singe	to burn slightly: to scorch on the surface.
single	1. only one: a **single** game.
	2. not married: a **single** man.
singly	one at a time.
sink	1. to go down slowly.
	2. a large bowl for washing dishes in a kitchen.
sip	to drink in tiny amounts.

sir	1. the title of a knight.
	2. a title of respect.
siren	a warning whistle which can be heard for a long distance.
sister	1. a girl who has the same parents as ourselves.
	2. the nurse in charge of a ward in a hospital.
sit	to be seated.
site	the ground where something is built or is going to be built.
six	6. a number, five and one added together.
	I was **sixth** in the test.
sixteen	16. a number, six and ten added together.
sixty	60. a number, six tens.
size	how big something is.
skate	to move on ice with boots fitted with a metal blade, or with small rollers.
skeleton	the bones of the body of an animal or a person.
sketch	to draw quickly and roughly.
skid	to slide out of control on a slippery surface.
skill	cleverness: ability to do something properly.
	The boy rode his bicycle in a **skilful** manner.
skin	the outer covering of a person, animal or of a fruit.
skip	to jump over a turning rope.
skipper	the captain of a ship.
skirt	a woman's dress which hangs from the waist.
skittle	a wooden block knocked down by throwing or rolling a ball.

skull	the top bones of the head.
sky	where the sun, moon and stars are seen.
skylark	a small bird noted for its song when it is flying high in the sky.
slab	a thick flat piece of something.
slack	1. loose: sagging. 2. careless: idle.
slacks	trousers.
slam	to bang something purposely.
slant	a slope: a gradual rise.
slap	a hard smack with the flat hand.
slate	1. a grey rock. 2. a writing board. 3. a thin tile used on roofs.
slaughter	to kill many people or animals at one time.
slave	a person forced to work without payment. **Slavery** was stopped many years ago.
slay	to kill: to murder.
sledge	1. a small carriage which will move smoothly on snow. 2. a heavy hammer such as that used by a blacksmith.
sleep	to rest peacefully with the eyes closed. The hot room made us feel quite **sleepy.**
sleet	snow and rain falling together.
sleeve	the part of a garment that covers the arms.
sleigh	a sledge drawn by animals.
slender	long and thin: slim.
slice	a thin piece cut from a larger piece.
slide	1. to move smoothly along a slippery surface: to slip. 2. a hair-fastener used by girls and ladies.
slight	small: thin.
slightly	a little: a small amount. She was **slightly** taller than I was.
slim	tall and thin.
sling	1. a bandage made for a broken arm. 2. to throw: to swing.
slink	to creep about so that others do not see.
slip	1. to lose our balance on a smooth surface. The road was quite **slippery.** 2. to make a mistake.
slippers	light shoes worn in the house.
slit	a tear: a narrow cut.
slope	a slant: something that is higher at one end than the other.
slow	not quick: taking a long time. We walked **slowly** through the gate.
slug	a garden snail without a shell.
slumber	to sleep: to be at rest.

sly	cunning: unable to be trusted: crafty. The fox looked **slyly** into the farmyard.
smack	1. a hit with the flat hand. 2. a small fishing-boat.
small	little: not important.
smart	1. clever: quick to understand. 2. neat, clean and tidy in our dress. 3. to sting.
smartly	1. quickly. 2. brightly.
smash	to break into several pieces: to crash.
smear	to make something dirty, sticky or greasy.
smell	to sniff with the nose.
smile	to laugh: to show amusement on our faces.
smite	to hit hard.
smith	a man, like a **blacksmith,** who makes and repairs things made of metal.
smoke	1. the dark cloud which rises from something which is burning. The air round the chimney was **smoky.** 2. to burn tobacco in a pipe or cigarette. The man was **smoking** his pipe.
smooth	flat: even: not rough. The boat sailed **smoothly** across the harbour.
smother	to stop someone from breathing by covering the mouth and nose.
smoulder	to burn slowly with no flame but with plenty of smoke.
smudge	to make a dirty mark: to smear.
smuggle	to take things into a country without paying a tax on them. The cave was at one time used by **smugglers.**
smut	a spot of soot or dirt.
snail	a small animal which lives in gardens and has its shell on its back.
snake	a serpent: a legless animal which glides on its body.
snap	1. to bite at something quickly. 2. to break something with a crack. 3. to crack the fingers.
snare	a trap set to catch animals.
snarl	1. to show the teeth when growling. The dog **snarled.** 2. to speak in an angry way.
snatch	to grab a thing quickly.
sneak	1. to move secretly. 2. to betray somebody. 3. a person who cannot be trusted.
sneer	to speak with scorn.
sneeze	a sudden noisy rush of air from the nose.
sniff	to smell noisily with quick breaths.

snob	a person who thinks too much about money and position.
snore	to breathe heavily and noisily when asleep.
snow	frozen raindrops which fall in white flakes. Outside the window, the **snowflakes** were falling fast.
snowdrop	a tiny white flower seen in early spring.
snub	to show a person that he is not wanted by not speaking to him or not looking at him.
snug	warm, cosy and comfortable.
soak	to make very wet indeed: to drench.
soap	a substance which is made from fat and which is used with water to wash things. The water in the bath was **soapy.**
sob	to weep noisily.
sock	a woollen or cloth covering for the feet and ankles: a short stocking.
sod	a piece of grass or turf with its roots.
sofa	a settee: a seat for more than one person.
soft	1. gentle: mild. 2. not hard. 3. quiet: not loud. The music was played **softly.**

soil	1. the earth in which plants grow. 2. to make something dirty.
soldier	a warrior: a fighting man who belongs to an army.
sole	1. the bottom of the foot, or of the boots and shoes. 2. the only one. 3. a fish which is flat.
solemn	very serious.
solid	hard: not hollow.
solo	1. a piece of music played or sung by one person alone. 2. anything done by one person alone. He was riding a **solo** motor-cycle.
solve	to find the answer.
some	a few: not all.
somersault	to turn over and over, head over heels.
something	a certain thing about which we are not clear.
son	a male child.
song	music made by the voice.
soon	shortly: before long.
sooner	earlier.
soot	the black substance found in chimneys and which is caused by smoke.
sore	1. painful: sharp. 2. a place on the body which is painful.
sorrow	pity: sadness. When we heard what had happened, we were all **sorrowful.**

sorry	full of pity and regret.
sort	1. a kind: a type. 2. to pick out certain ones.
soul	the spirit: the part of a person that lives on.
sound	1. a noise: something that we hear. 2. strong and healthy.
soup	the food which is made when meat or vegetables have been boiled in water.
sour	1. bitter to taste. 2. bad-tempered: surly.
source	the start: the beginning. The **source** of the river was in the mountains.
south	the opposite to the north. She came from a **southern** district.
sovereign	1. a gold coin worth one pound when it was made. 2. a king or queen: a ruler.
sow	(like 'low') to set seeds so that they will grow.
sow	(like 'now') a female pig.
space	1. the distance between things. 2. beyond the earth.
spade	a tool which is used for digging soil.
spare	1. not in use at present: extra. I took a **spare** pair of shoes. 2. to give up: to do without. I can **spare** some sweets.
spark	a tiny burning bit.
sparkle	to glitter. We saw the frost **sparkle** in the moonlight.
sparrow	a small, brown bird often seen near to houses.
speak	to talk: to use the voice. The people became quiet as the **speaker** rose to his feet.
spear	a sharp, pointed weapon with a long, thin handle.
special	of a particular or different kind. Mother made a **special** cake for the party.
speck	a tiny spot of something.
spectacle	an unusual sight: a show.
spectacles	glasses for the eyes to help us to see better.
spectator	one who watches something that is taking place.
speech	1. the sound we make when we speak. 2. a special talk by one person to other people.
speed	quickness in moving.
spell	1. to arrange letters to make words. We must be careful with our **spelling.** 2. magic words.
spend	1. to give money to buy something. 2. to use time in doing something.
sphere	a round ball: a globe.
spice	something such as pepper used to give food a special taste.

spider	an eight-legged animal which weaves a web to catch insects for food.
spike	a pointed piece of metal.
spill	1. to upset: to tip over. 2. a splinter of wood or a piece of paper used to carry a light.
spin	1. to turn round and round quickly. 2. to make cotton or wool into thread.
spinster	an unmarried woman.
spire	the pointed upper part of a church steeple.
spirit	1. the soul of a person. 2. life: energy. 3. strong drink. 4. a ghost.
splash	1. to throw or to scatter water. 2. the sound made by falling water.
splendid	excellent: grand. The team played **splendidly.**
splendour	great beauty: glory.
splinter	a small sharp piece: a fragment.
split	to crack: to break something down the middle.
spoil	1. to ruin or to damage something. 2. things which have been stolen by using force.
spoke	a thin bar from the centre to the rim of a wheel.
sponge	1. a soft substance which soaks up water. His mother was **sponging** the cut. 2. a soft cake.
spoon	a utensil which we use when we are eating.
sport	games or pastimes usually played outside.
spot	1. a tiny mark. 2. to notice something.
spout	a tube through which liquid is poured from kettles and teapots.
sprawl	to spread out the limbs lazily.
spray	1. a tiny bunch of flowers. 2. thin jets of water.
spread	1. to take up more space. 2. to scatter things about.
spring	1. to jump through the air. 2. a metal coil. 3. where water appears from below the ground. 4. one of the seasons.
sprinkle	to scatter water in small drops.
sprint	to run quickly for a short distance.
spy	1. a person who helps the enemy. 2. to see something secretly.
squabble	to quarrel noisily and in a childish way.

squall	a sudden storm of wind.
square	a drawing with four equal sides.
squash	to crush: to squeeze tightly together.
squeak	a small, sharp noise like that made by a mouse.
squeal	a howl: a long, sharp cry often caused by either pain or joy.
squeeze	to press together: to squash. He tried to **squeeze** the balloon to burst it.
squire	a country landowner.
squirm	to twist about: to wriggle.
squirrel	a small, wild animal which has a bushy tail and which lives among the trees.
squirt	to send out a jet of water.
stab	to make a hole with a sharp, pointed tool.
stable	a building where horses are kept.
staff	1. a long stick or pole. 2. people who work in such places as offices or schools.
stag	a male deer which has large horns.
stage	1. a platform for acting. 2. a part of a journey.
stagger	to sway as we walk.
stain	1. a mark which spoils something. 2. a dye which is often used on wood.
stair	steps which lead to another floor in a building. Along the **staircase** a carpet was laid.
stake	a strong, pointed post.
stale	old: no longer fit to eat.
stalk	1. the stem of a flower or plant. 2. to track an animal quietly.
stall	1. a counter for selling things. 2. a place where a horse is kept. 3. a seat in a part of a picture-house or theatre.
stammer	to stutter: to speak with jumbled words.
stamp	1. a postage stamp which is stuck on to a letter or a parcel to pay the postage. 2. to make a noise with the foot. 3. to make a mark by pressing.
stand	1. to be upright on the feet. 2. seats under cover at a sports ground. 3. a platform on which things are shown.
standard	1. a level or example to be reached. 2. a flag.

star	1. a speck of light in the sky at night. The winter's night was clear and **starry.** 2. an important actor.
starch	a white substance mixed with water to stiffen clothes.
stare	to look at something steadily for a long time.
start	1. to begin. 2. to make a sudden movement.
startle	to frighten or to surprise someone.
starve	to be ill or dying because we are without food. The people were suffering from **starvation.**
state	1. to say in words, either by writing or by speaking. 2. a part of a country. 3. the condition of something. Her clothes were in a poor **state.**
statement	what has been said or written.
station	1. a place from which trains or buses begin or stop on a journey. 2. a fixed place: a **police station.** Something which does not move may be said to be **stationary.**
stationer	a person who sells writing materials. Notepaper and envelopes are called **stationery.**

statue	an image: a likeness in wood or stone.
stay	to remain: not to go away.
steady **steadily**	firm: not moving. evenly. The boat moved **steadily** towards the harbour.
steal	1. to rob: to take something that is not ours. 2. to move quietly and secretly.
steam	the vapour that comes from boiling water.
steamer	a boat which is driven by steam. The **steamer** took the people round the bay.
steed	a horse which carries a rider.
steel	a hard and strong metal which is made from iron.
steep	sloping sharply. We walked up a **steep** hill.
steeple	a pointed tower on a church. A man who works at great heights is called a **steeplejack.**
steer	1. to guide a boat or a motor-car. 2. a bullock.
stem	1. the stalk which bears the leaves on a plant. 2. to stop: to check.
step	1. a pace forward or backward. 2. the stone slab in front of a door. 3. the part of a staircase on which we tread.
stern	1. firm: harsh. 2. the back part of a boat.

stew	meat with vegetables boiled slowly in water.	**stone**	1. a piece of rock. The path up which we went was **stony.** 2. a hard seed in fruit. 3. a precious jewel.
stick	1. a short piece of wood. 2. to fasten by using gum or glue.		
sticky	1. able to be stuck. 2. like gum or paste.	**stool**	a seat without a back.
stiff	straight: difficult to bend. The soldiers stood **stiffly** to attention.	**stoop**	to bend the body forward.
		stop	to halt from doing what we have been doing. Fog caused a **stoppage** of flying from the airport.
stile	steps by which we can climb easily over a fence or wall.	**stopper**	a cork or plug from a bottle.
still	quiet: peaceful: not moving.	**store**	1. a shop. 2. to save things to use later.
sting	a painful stab from an insect or plant.		
stingy	mean: not generous.	**storey**	the rooms on one floor of a building. The new flats were ten **storeys** high.
stir	1. to move something round and round with a stick or spoon. 2. to begin to move about. The blowing of the wind **stirred** the leaves.		
		stork	a large water-bird with long legs and a long straight beak.
		storm	1. rough weather. The boat sailed safely through the **stormy** seas. 2. to rage at someone.
stirrup	metal rings into which a horse rider puts his feet.		
stitch	to sew with needle and thread.	**story**	a tale. Young children like to hear fairy **stories.**
stock	a quantity of things or animals.	**stout**	fat: thick.
stocking	a silky or woollen covering for the legs and feet.	**stove**	a closed fire-place used for cooking.
stoke	to put fuel on to a fire. The **stoker** was lighting the boiler.	**straight**	1. direct: without a turning. 2. tidy and neat.
stomach	the part of the body into which the food goes after being eaten.	**strain**	1. to pull hard. 2. to hurt a muscle.

strait	a narrow place: the **Straits** of Dover.
strange	unusual: remarkable.
stranger	a person who does not know the district. As he was a **stranger,** he had to ask the way.
strap	a long, thin piece of leather.
straw	the dried stem of corn after the grain has been taken away.
strawberry	a soft red fruit.
stray	to wander away: to lose the way.
stream	1. a small river. 2. a crowd of people moving steadily along.
street	a road with buildings along its sides.
strength	power: being strong. The rope was doubled to **strengthen** it.
stretch	1. to make longer or wider by pulling. 2. to reach out.
stretcher	a covered frame to carry an injured person who is lying down.
strict	firm: severe.
stride	a long pace or step.
strike	1. to hit something hard: to smite. 2. to chime. 3. to light a match by rubbing it.
string	thin cord.

strip	1. a long, narrow length of material such as cloth or paper. 2. to undress: to uncover.
stripe	a narrow mark or line of a different colour.
stroke	to pass the hand gently over something.
stroll	to walk along slowly.
strong	mighty: powerful.
struggle	to try very hard to do something.
student	a person who studies: a pupil.
study	1. to try to learn. 2. a room in which we try to learn.
stuff	1. things: materials. 2. to fill something with packing. Mother **stuffed** feathers into the cushions.
stumble	to trip: to fall.
stump	1. the part of the tree which is left when the tree has been cut down. 2. an upright stick used in cricket to bowl at.
stun	to strike a person until he is senseless.
stupid	foolish: silly. We were surprised at his **stupidity.**
sturdy	strong: well-built: healthy.
stutter	to stammer.

sty
1. a place where pigs are kept.
2. a painful, small boil on the eyelid.

style a way of doing something.

subject
1. a person who obeys orders.
2. what we are talking about.

submarine a warship which can sail under water.

submit to give in: to yield.

substance something of which things are made.

subtract to take away one thing from another.
Subtraction sums are taught at school.

succeed to manage to do what we try to do.
We were pleased at his **success.**
He was **successful** in his work.

such of that sort.

suck to take something into the mouth by breathing inwards.

sudden quick: not expected.
Suddenly the light went out.

suet the hard fat which is found in meat.

suffer
1. to allow.
2. to have great pain.
Accidents often cause much **suffering.**

sufficient enough: as much as is needed.

sugar a sweet substance which is made from sugar canes or beet.

suggest to advise somebody what to do: to hint.
He was pleased that his **suggestion** had helped.

suit
1. a set of clothes.
2. to please.

suitable correct: of the right sort.
We did not think that her dress was **suitable** for the occasion.

sulk to be bad tempered because we do not get our own way.
Sulky people are not liked.

sultan an eastern chief.

sum
1. something to be worked with figures.
2. to add numbers and find the total.

summer the warmest season of the year, the opposite to winter.

summit the top: the highest point.

summon to call: to make someone attend.

sun the heavenly body which gives us light and warmth.
We had wonderful **sunshine** at the seaside.
The day dawned bright and **sunny** and ended with a glorious **sunset.**
Sunrise over the sea is a beautiful sight.

supper the last meal of the day.

supply
1. a quantity or a store of things.
2. to provide the things that are needed.

support	1. to help someone by giving what is needed. 2. to hold up. 3. to provide for.
suppose	to think: to believe something to be true.
sure	certain. As the skies darkened, we knew that it would **surely** rain.
surface	the outside or the top of something.
surgeon	a doctor who performs operations.
surly	bad tempered and rude.
surname	our last name: the family name.
surprise	a shock: something that we did not expect.
surrender	to give in: to stop fighting.
surround	to be all round: to enclose.
swallow	1. to take in something through the throat. 2. a small bird with a forked tail.
swamp	marsh: wet ground.
swan	a large water-bird with a long neck.
swarm	a large number of insects moving together.
sway	to move from side to side.
swear	1. to promise faithfully that we will do something. 2. to use bad words.
sweat	1. moisture coming through the skin. 2. to perspire.
sweep	1. to clean something with a brush. 2. a man who cleans chimneys.
sweet	1. pleasant to taste: like sugar. 2. a piece of chocolate, toffee, or something similar. 3. kind: helpful.
swell	1. to become bigger. 2. large unbroken waves.
swelling	a part which becomes bigger.
swelter	to feel uncomfortable because we are too hot: to sweat.
swerve	to move sideways quickly.
swift	1. very speedy: very fast. 2. a bird like a swallow.
swill	to wash something clean with water.
swim	to move along in water by using the arms and legs. He was an excellent **swimmer.**
swing	1. to sway: to move round. 2. a moving seat on ropes.
switch	1. an instrument for making electrical things work. 2. a thin cane.
sword	a sharp-sided, metal weapon like a long, two-sided knife.
sycamore	a tree with large leaves.
syllable	a part of a word which can be pronounced by itself.
syrup	sugar boiled in water to make a thick, sweet liquid.

H

T

tabby	a female cat.
table	1. a flat piece of furniture which stands on legs. 2. a list of facts in order.
tablet	1. a cake of soap. 2. a pill of medicine. 3. a small piece of paper, flat wood or stone used for writing purposes.
tack	1. a small nail with a large head. 2. to fasten things together by using long stitches. 3. to change the direction of a sailing-boat.
tackle	1. to try to do something. 2. the things which are necessary to do something. The man was carrying his fishing **tackle**.
tadpole	a young frog or toad just hatched out of its egg.
tag	a luggage label.
tail	the part of an animal which sticks out at the back.
tailor	a person who makes clothes such as suits and coats.
take	to receive something.
tale	a story.
talent	ability: what a person is able to do well.

talk	to speak: to say. The children were very **talkative**.
tall	higher than usual.
tame	not wild: friendly.
tamper	to interfere: to meddle.
tan	1. a light brown colour. 2. to make skins into leather. Skins are made into leather at the **tannery**.
tandem	a two-seater bicycle.
tangle	a jumble: a muddle.
tank	1. a container to hold large amounts of liquid. 2. a large machine which is used in war and is able to move over very rough country.
tanker	a boat which carries petrol and oil. Oil was being taken from the **tanker** at the dock.
tap	1. a knob which is turned to allow liquids to flow. 2. a tiny knock.
tape	a narrow piece of cloth.
taper	1. a thin piece of wax candle. 2. to become thin at one end.
tapestry	pictures or patterns in silk or cotton worked on heavy cloth.
tar	a thick, black liquid made from coal.
target	something at which we aim.

tarnish	when metal grows dull because it needs cleaning.
tarry	to stay for a short time on the way.
tart	1. a small pastry having jam or fruit in it. 2. sour to the taste.
tartan	a woollen cloth with a pattern of stripes and squares which is often used for making kilts in Scotland.
task	a job: work which has to be done.
tassel	a hanging bunch of threads often used as a decoration.
taste	flavour.
tasty	having a pleasant flavour. The plate was covered with **tasty** cakes.
tavern	an inn: a public house.
tax	money which has to be paid to the government by the people.
taxi	a motor-car that can be hired.
tea	a hot drink made from the leaves of the tea plant.
teach	to give lessons. At school, we are **taught** many subjects. The **teacher** was **teaching** a new song.
team	1. a number of people who work or play together. 2. a number of animals working together.
tear	(say 'teer') a water-drop from the eyes.
tear	(say 'tare') to rip: to pull apart.
tease	to make fun of somebody: to annoy.
teem	1. to pour: to rain heavily. 2. to swarm.
telegram	a message sent quickly by the post office.
telegraph	a means of sending messages quickly by using machines driven by electricity.
telephone	a way of speaking to another person by using a machine worked by electric wires.
telescope	special glasses through which distant things seem larger and clearer.
television	seeing pictures by wireless.
tell	to say: to give news.
temper	1. the state of the mind: the mood we are in. 2. when we are angry or annoyed about something that has happened.
temperature	warmth or coldness.
tempest	a very bad storm of wind and rain.
temple	1. a large church. 2. the part of the head between the forehead and the ear.
tempt	to persuade someone to try to do what they really do not wish to do or ought not to do. The snow in the playground was a **temptation** to the boys.

ten	10. a number, two fives.
tend	1. to look after. 2. to lean towards.
tender	1. gentle: kind. 2. a coal truck behind a railway engine.
tennis	a game played by two or four people with a ball and with rackets.
tenor	a man able to sing high notes.
tent	a waterproof shelter placed over poles and held by ropes.
term	1. a period of time. 2. a part of the school year.
terminus	the end of a railway or bus journey.
terrace	1. a flat, raised piece of ground. 2. a row of houses.
terrible	causing fear: dreadful.
terrier	a small dog.
terrify	to frighten: to fill with fear.
territory	a large area of land.
terror	great fear: great fright.
test	to examine: to try out.
tether	to fasten an animal by means of a rope.
text	1. a part of a book just as it was written. 2. words taken from the Bible.
than	a word used to compare. I am older **than** you are.
thank	to say that we are grateful. We were **thankful** to see them arrive safely.
that	1. one of two, this or **that**. 2. a word showing which one we are talking about.
thatch	a dried, straw covering for a roof.
thaw	warm weather which melts snow and ice.
theatre	1. a building where plays are acted. 2. a room in a hospital where special treatment takes place.
theft	stealing or robbing.
their(s)	belonging to them. They left **their** coats.
then	1. at that time. 2. after that.
there	at, or in, that place. It was **there** that I saw it happen.
thermometer	an instrument to measure heat and cold (temperature).
they	those we are talking about.
thick	1. wide: fat: deep. We measured the **thickness** of the ice. 2. dense. The fog began to **thicken**.
thief	a person who steals. The policemen went after the two **thieves**.
thigh	the part of the leg between the body and the knee.
thimble	a metal cap which is worn on the finger when we are using a needle.
thin	not fat: narrow: lean.

thing	an object.
think	to believe: to use the mind.
third	the one which comes after the second one.
thirst	the wish to drink. The long walk made everybody **thirsty.**
thirteen	13. a number, ten and three added together.
thirty	30. a number, three tens.
this	a word showing which one we mean. **This** is the one.
thistle	a wild plant with prickly leaves and purple flowers.
thorn	a prickle or point on a plant stem. The path over the fields was rough and **thorny.**
thorough	1. taking great care. 2. complete. We knew that the map was **thoroughly** reliable.
though	even if.
thought	an idea: a plan in the mind. It was **thoughtful** of her to send a present.
thousand	1000. a number, ten hundreds.
thread	1. strong cotton used in sewing. 2. to put cotton through the eye of a needle.
threat	when we say that we intend to harm or to punish someone.
threaten	to promise to harm or to punish someone.
three	3. a number, two and one added together.
thrifty	careful with money and with things, taking care not to waste anything.
thrilling	exciting.
thrive	to grow bigger and stronger.
throat	the front part of the neck: the part of the mouth with which we swallow.
throb	a strong, steady beat.
throne	a special chair of state for a king or a queen.
throng	a crowd of people pressed together.
through	from one side to the other: from one end to the other.
throw	to hurl something away.
thrush	a brown bird noted for its song.
thrust	to push hard.
thud	the noise of something falling or bumping heavily.
thumb	the shortest and thickest finger of the hand.
thump	a heavy blow, usually struck with the fist.
thunder	the crash of noise that follows lightning.
tick	1. a mark to show that something has been checked. 2. the sound made by a watch or clock.
ticket	a card or paper allowing us to go into a place or to travel by train or bus.
tickle	to touch someone lightly and so to make him laugh.

tide	the rising and falling of the sea twice during each day.
tidings	news.
tidy	neat and in good order: properly arranged.
tie	1. a narrow piece of cloth worn round the neck. 2. to make a knot. 3. to be equal in a test.
tiger	a fierce, wild animal which has black stripes on a yellow skin.
tight	fitting closely together. His hands were fastened together **tightly.**
tile	a flat piece of hard-baked clay used on roofs and to make fireplaces.
till	1. until. 2. to dig land. 3. a drawer for holding money in a shop.
tilt	to lean: to bend over.
timber	wood which is made ready to use for such things as making furniture.
time	1. the hour by the clock. 2. the right beat in music. 3. a period.
timid	easily frightened: likely to be afraid.
tin	1. a shiny, white metal. 2. a metal can.
tingle	a prickly feeling often caused by cold or excitement.
tinkle	the sound made by small bells.
tinsel	glittering material used for decoration.
tint	the shade of a colour.
tiny	very small indeed.
tip	1. the pointed end of something. 2. to upset something. 3. to give money for something done.
tit	a tiny bird.
title	1. the name of a book, a play or a piece of music. 2. the first part of a name to show rank: **Lord** Nelson.
titter	to giggle: to laugh quietly.
to	towards: come **to me.**
toad	an animal which is like a frog.
toast	warmed, crisp bread which has been browned by heat. The **toaster** was placed on the table.
tobacco	the name of a plant from which the leaves are taken and used for smoking.
today	this day.
toddle	to walk with short steps as a baby does.
toe	one of the five end parts of the foot.
toffee	a sticky sweet made from sugar and butter.
together	1. with each other. 2. at the same time.
toil	hard work.

toilet	a room for washing.	**torch**	1. an electric light which can be carried about. 2. a burning stick carried to give light.
toll	1. the slow ringing of a large bell. 2. a charge to use a private road or bridge.	**torment**	1. great pain and suffering. 2. to tease, annoy or cause pain to someone.
tomato	a soft, round, red fruit.	**torpedo**	a shell which is fired through water, usually against ships.
tomb	a grave.		
tomorrow	the day after today.	**torrent**	a violent stream of water: a very fast-flowing river.
ton	a measure of weight.		
tone	the sound of the voice used in speaking or singing: the sound of a musical instrument.	**tortoise**	a slow-moving animal covered by a shell.
		torture	to cause great pain to someone purposely.
tongs	pincers for picking lumps of coal or lumps of sugar.	**toss**	to throw something into the air.
tongue	1. a part of the mouth used for tasting. 2. the language spoken.	**total**	everything added together: the whole.
		totter	to stagger: to stand or to move unsteadily.
tonight	the night of today.		
tonne	1000 kilogrammes.	**touch**	to feel gently.
tonsil	a part of the back of the throat.	**tough**	hard: strong: not easy to bite or to cut.
too	1. also. I shall go **too.** 2. more than is usual. The grass was **too** wet.	**tour**	a journey from one place to other places.
		tow	to drag: to pull along using a rope or a chain.
tool	an instrument used to help us to do some work.	**towards**	in the direction of.
tooth	strong bones from the jaw which we use for biting food. When we have **toothache,** we go to the dentist.	**towel**	a piece of cloth for drying wet things.
		tower	a tall, narrow building high above the ground.
top	1. the highest point: above all others. 2. a toy which spins.	**town**	a small city or a large village.
topple	to fall over.	**toy**	a plaything.

trace	1. a small amount left behind. 2. to copy exactly. 3. to find after searching.
track	1. a narrow path. 2. a racecourse. 3. a railway line. 4. to trail someone.
tractor	a strong machine used for towing heavy loads.
trade	1. the work that we do. 2. buying and selling. The **trader** was buying for his shops.
traffic	movement of vehicles and people.
tragedy	an unhappy event: a disaster.
trail	1. to follow a track or the scent. 2. to move along slowly at the back. The lorry was pulling a **trailer.**
train	1. railway coaches joined to an engine. 2. part of a dress which trails on the ground. 3. to prepare for a competition. The boys were **training** for the final game.
traitor	a person who tells secret things to the enemy and betrays his country.
tram	a passenger car which runs on rails usually through the streets.
tramp	1. a long walk. 2. a wandering beggar. 3. to walk heavily. We should be careful not to **trample** on growing crops.
trance	a very deep dream.
transfer	1. to move things or people from one place to another. 2. a picture that can be moved from a paper on to something else.
translate	to give the same meaning in another language.
transmit	to send along: to pass a message, often by wireless.
transparent	able to be seen through. Glass is usually **transparent.**
transport	to move goods or people from place to place.
trap	1. a way to catch animals. The **trapper** was carrying the animal's skin. 2. to catch something in a clever way.
travel	to move about from place to place. The **traveller** was sailing round the world.
trawler	a fishing boat which catches fish by dragging a large net.
tray	a flat piece of board or metal for carrying small articles.
treacle	syrup: a sweet liquid made from sugar.
tread	to move on foot.

treadle	the part of a machine moved by the foot to make the machine work. The sewing machine was worked by a **treadle.**
treason	when a country or a king is betrayed by a traitor.
treasure	something of great value.
treasurer	the person who looks after the money which belongs to a group of people. The **treasurer** paid the bills.
treat	1. a special, happy event. 2. to make a gift. 3. how we act towards people. We received excellent **treatment.**
tree	a large plant with a trunk, branches and leaves.
tremble	to shiver: to shake with excitement, fear or cold.
trench	a ditch dug in the earth for a special purpose.
trespass	to go into private places. The notice said, 'Trespassers will be prosecuted'.
trestle	a stand for a table.
trial	1. a test. 2. an examination before a judge.
triangle	a three-sided figure.
tribe	a group of people ruled by one chief.
trick	1. to surprise and amuse people. 2. to cheat other people.
trickle	a gentle flow of water.
tricycle	a cycle having three wheels.

trier	a person who tries.
trifle	1. a small thing of no importance. 2. a cake mixed with cream.
trigger	a small lever which is pulled to fire a gun.
trim	1. tidy: neat. 2. to cut and make tidy.
trio	a group of three people doing something together.
trip	1. a pleasure outing. 2. to stumble and fall.
triumph	a victory. The winning team was given a **triumphant** welcome.
trivial	of little importance.
trolley	a small handcart.
trolley-bus	a bus driven by electricity carried by overhead wires.
troop	1. a number of soldiers. 2. a group of people.
tropics	part of the world near to the equator. The hunters were caught in a **tropical** storm.
trot	to run gently with short steps.
trouble	1. a worry: a problem. 2. to bother: to annoy.
trough	a stone or metal container used to hold food and water for animals.
trousers	clothing for the legs and the lower part of the body.
trout	a fresh-water fish rather like a small salmon.

trowel	a small spade used by gardeners.
truant	a person who is absent from duty without permission.
truck	a waggon for carrying heavy goods.
trudge	to walk slowly and heavily as we do when we are tired.
true	correct: honest. It was a **truly** great victory.
trumpet	a brass wind instrument.
trunk	1. the stem of a tree. 2. a large box for carrying clothes. 3. an elephant's long nose.
trust	1. to believe to be true. 2. to rely on. We knew from what she did that she was quite **trustworthy.**
truth	what is true. **Truthful** people can always be trusted.
try	1. to attempt. We **tried** to win. 2. to test. The man **tried** the car before he bought it.
tub	a barrel with an open top.
tube	1. a pipe made of rubber, glass or metal. 2. an underground railway in large cities such as London.
tuck	to fold close together.
tuft	a bunch of grass, hair or feathers.
tug	1. to pull: to tow. 2. a powerful boat used to pull other boats.
tulip	a flower grown from a bulb and shaped like a bell.
tumble	to fall heavily.
tumbler	a drinking glass.
tumult	a noisy disturbance.
tune	a number of pleasant musical notes. The choir sang a **tuneful** song.
tunic	a short coat or cloak.
tunnel	a long covered passage-way through hills or under rivers.
turban	an Eastern head-covering made from a long strip of material wound round the head.
turf	short grass and the earth in which it grows.
turkey	a large bird used as food.
turn	1. to face a different way. 2. to swing round. We came to a **turning** in the path.
turnip	a root vegetable which is shaped like a ball and is brown in colour.
turret	a small tower in a building.
tusk	a long, pointed tooth or bone found in certain animals such as elephants.
tutor	a teacher.

twain	two.
tweed	rough, woollen cloth used for suits and heavy coats.
tweezers	small pincers used for moving tiny things.
twelve	12. a number, ten and two added together. December is the **twelfth** month of the year.
twenty	20. a number, two tens: a score. We live at the **twentieth** house in the road.
twig	a small branch of a tree.
twilight	the half-light at sunset and sunrise.
twin	one of two children born at the same time.
twine	1. thin, strong string. 2. to wrap round. The weeds were **twined** round the tree.
twinkle	1. to gleam: to glitter. 2. a gleam from the eyes.
twirl	to twist round: to spin quickly.
twist	to wind: to turn.
twitter	the chirping sound made by birds.
two	2. a number, one and one added together.
type	1. sort: kind. 2. letters used to print books. The girl was using a **typewriter.**
tyrant	a cruel ruler.
tyre	the rubber round the outside of a wheel.

U

ugly	not pleasing to look at.
umbrella	a covering which can be shut or opened to keep off the rain.
umpire	a judge at a game: a referee.
un - - -	the letters 'un' in front of a word often mean 'not'. This will be noticed in some of the words which follow.
uncle	the brother of father or mother: an aunt's husband.
unconscious	not conscious: not knowing what is happening.
under	below: beneath. The stool was **underneath** the table.
understand	to know what something means: to know all about something.
undertake	to agree to do something.
undo	to unfasten.
undone	not fastened.
unfair	not fair.
unhappy	not happy.
uniform	1. special clothing worn by all people of the same class such as policemen, firemen, sailors, soldiers and airmen. 2. exactly alike.
union	a joining together of two or more things.
unite	to join together into one.
universe	all things that exist.
university	a place of learning for older students.
unkind	not kind.
unless	if not: except.

unload	to take off the load.
unpleasant	not pleasant.
unruly	out of control.
until	up to the time of: till.
untruth	a lie: an untrue saying.
unwell	not well.
up	to a higher place.
upon	on.
upper	the higher part.
upright	1. standing straight up: erect. 2. honest and trustworthy.
uproar	a noisy quarrel: a riot.
upset	1. to turn over: to knock down. 2. to make others unhappy.
upwards	up to a higher place.
urge	to press somebody to do a certain thing: to push: to beg.
urgent	of great importance: needing to be dealt with at once.
use	to do something with.
useful	of some use.
useless	of no use.
usual	often done: common. We **usually** walk when we go to school.
utensil	a useful tool or container.
utmost	1. the most that is possible. 2. the greatest.
utter	to speak: to state.
utterly	quite: absolutely. It was **utterly** impossible for us to do as he asked.

V

vacant	empty: with nothing inside.
vacation	a holiday.
vagabond	a wanderer: a beggar.
vague	not certain: not sure.
vain	1. proud: conceited. 2. useless. We begged them not to go, but our words were **in vain.**
vale	a valley.
valiant	noble: brave.
valley	low ground between two hills.
valour	bravery: courage.
value	worth: price: importance. The lady was wearing a **valuable** ring.
valve	1. a part in a wireless or a television set. 2. an instrument to control a flow of water or air. The **valve** in the bicycle tyre was useless.
van	1. a covered lorry. 2. a railway luggage coach.
vane	an instrument to show the direction of the wind.
vanish	to go out of sight: to disappear. The ship **vanished** into the mist.
vanity	pride: conceit.
vapour	mist, steam or cloud.
variety	many different things mixed together.

various	different. We were shown **various** dresses from which to choose.
varnish	a substance put on to paint to make it hard and shiny.
vary	to alter: to change.
vase	a container used for holding flowers.
vast	of great size: very large.
vault	1. a cellar. 2. to jump over something.
veer	to change direction: to swerve.
vegetable	a plant which is grown for food.
vehicle	something which moves such as a cart, car, van or sledge and which is used for carrying people or goods.
veil	a covering to hide something.
vein	a tube which carries blood round the body: a blood-vessel.
velvet	smooth, soft, thick and silky cloth.
venture	to dare to go: to run a risk.
verandah	a covered balcony at the front or side of a building.
verb	a doing word.
verdict	what is decided at a trial: whether a person is guilty or not guilty.
verge	the edge: the border.
verily	truly: actually.

vermin	small animals and insects which do harm.
verse	1. poetry. 2. a group of lines from a poem. 3. a small section from the Bible.
version	a special account of what has happened.
vertical	perfectly straight up.
very	real: true.
vessel	1. a container to hold liquids. 2. a ship.
vest	clothing worn next to the body.
vestry	a room in a church.
vet	an animal doctor: a veterinary surgeon.
veterinary	to do with the illness of animals.
vex	to annoy: to disappoint. We were **vexed** that we had not been told.
vibrate	to throb: to shake. We could feel the **vibration** of the ship's engine.
vicar	a clergyman: a parish priest.
vice	1. evil: wickedness. 2. a tool which grips things to prevent them from moving.
victim	one who has suffered because of what other people have done to him or because of illness.

victor	the winner of a battle or of a competition. The people cheered when they heard of the **victory.**
view	1. what we can see. 2. to look at something carefully.
vigour	strength: energy. Many games are **vigorous** exercise.
vile	mean: evil: horrible.
villa	a country house.
village	a number of houses grouped together: a small town.
villain	a wicked person: a rascal.
vine	a plant on which grapes grow.
vinegar	a sour liquid used for flavouring and for preserving food.
vineyard	a place where many vines are growing together.
violence	great force: rough treatment. Towards evening, a **violent** storm arose.
violet	1. a tiny bluish-purple flower. 2. a bluish-purple colour.
violin	a stringed musical instrument held under the chin and played with a bow.
viper	a small, poisonous snake.
virtue	goodness.
visible	able to be seen.
vision	1. sight. 2. something seen in a dream: a spirit.
visit	to call to see someone. The **visitor** was taken to the concert.
vivid	brilliant: bright and clear.
vocabulary	the words we use in speaking and writing.
voice	the sound made by the mouth.
void	vacant: quite empty.
volcano	a mountain which throws out hot ashes, steam and flames.
volley	a number of guns fired together.
volume	1. a large quantity. 2. a book. 3. the space inside something.
voluntary	done freely and openly without being forced.
vomit	to be sick.
vote	to make a choice: to choose at an election.
vow	a solemn promise which we should keep.
vowel	the letter a, e, i, o or u.
voyage	a journey by sea or air.
vulgar	rude: not polite.
vulture	a large, powerful, flesh-eating bird.

W

waddle	to walk as a duck walks with short, swinging steps.
wade	to walk through shallow water.
wafer	a thin biscuit often eaten with ice cream.

wag	1. to move from side to side. 2. a person who tells jokes and funny stories.
wage	1. money given for work done. 2. to make war.
wagon **waggon**	1. a cart to carry heavy loads. 2. a railway truck.
waif	a homeless child in need of help.
wail	to cry in sorrow.
waist	the middle of the body just below the ribs.
wait	1. to stay. 2. to serve food to people. The **waiter** and the **waitress** were preparing the tables.
wake	1. to rouse from sleep. 2. the foam made in the sea by the movement of a ship.
walk	to move on the feet. We **walked** in step to the music.
wall	bricks or stones making part of a building or fence.
wallaby	a small kangaroo.
wallet	a small pocket-book or bag.
walnut	1. a tree that produces wood that is used for making furniture. 2. the nut of this tree.
walrus	a water animal like a large seal found in cold lands.
waltz	a graceful dance.
wan	looking pale and ill.
wand	a thin straight stick used by conjurors and fairies.
wander	to roam about. A gipsy is a **wanderer** without a settled home.
wane	to become smaller. Night by night, the moon began to **wane.**
want	to wish to have.
war	fighting between nations. The natives at one time were quite **warlike.** Fighting ships are called **warships.**
warble	to sing like a bird.
ward	1. a child that is cared for by people who are not its parents. 2. a room at a hospital.
warden	1. a watchman. 2. a man in charge.
warder	a man who looks after prisoners in a jail.
wardrobe	a cupboard for storing clothes.
warm	fairly hot.
warn	to tell beforehand of difficulty or danger. A red light is often a sign of **warning.**

warrior	a fighting man: a soldier.
wash	to make something clean with water. Mother **washed** the clothes yesterday.
wasp	an insect with black and yellow stripes which can give a painful sting.
waste	1. useless things. 2. to use without care. We must learn not to be **wasteful.**
watch	1. a small clock which can be carried on the wrist or in a pocket. 2. to look at carefully. 3. to guard.
watchman	a man who looks after a place.
water	the liquid that is made by rain and found in rivers and in the sea.
waterfall	a stream or river falling from a height. We sat beside a cooling **waterfall.**
waterproof	any material through which water cannot go.
wave	1. a ripple on water. 2. to move the hand and arm from side to side. 3. curls of the hair. The girl had **wavy** hair.
wax	1. a substance made by bees. 2. the material used to make candles.

way	1. how we do something. 2. a road or path. We sat by the **wayside** to eat our lunch.
we	ourselves: us.
weak	not strong.
wealth	great riches. The man had become **wealthy.**
weapon	something with which we fight.
wear	1. to put clothes on to our bodies. 2. to grow weaker by using. Clothes which have been worn for a long time show signs of **wear.**
weary	tired. We climbed **wearily** into bed.
weasel	a small animal which lives on birds and animals such as mice.
weather	the state of the air: wet, dry, hot or cold.
weave	to make cloth from threads.
web	1. the net made by a spider to catch flies. 2. thin skin between the toes of birds which live on water.
wed	to marry. The organ played the **wedding** march.
wedge	a piece of wood which is thinner at one end than the other.

weed	a wild plant which grows where it is not wanted.
week	seven days. Some papers are sold **weekly.**
weep	to cry: to make tears.
weigh	to find how heavy something is. The butcher told us the **weight** of the meat.
weird	strange.
welcome	to greet happily.
welfare	happiness: good health.
well	1. a deep hole holding water or oil. 2. in good health. 3. correctly: properly.
wellingtons	long rubber boots.
wend	to go: to move gently.
west	the direction where the sun sets.
wet	very damp: soaked.
whale	the largest sea animal.
whaler	a special boat used for hunting and killing whales.
wharf	a pier where ships are loaded and unloaded.
what	which: that. We were allowed to do **whatever** we wished.
wheat	corn used for flour.
wheel	1. a ring of wood or metal which turns on its centre. 2. to push something that is fitted with wheels.
when	at what time: at the time that. We play games **whenever** we have the chance.
where	at what place: whither.
whether	if: which of the two.
which	that: what.
whiff	a puff of wind, smoke or scent.
while	1. a space of time. 2. during the time.
whimper	to cry softly: to moan.
whine	a long, sad cry like the cry of a dog.
whip	1. a piece of thin leather or cord on a handle. 2. to beat.
whirl	to spin round quickly.
whiskers	hair on the face.
whisper	to speak quietly. We **whispered** at the back of the cave.
whistle	1. a high, shrill note made by blowing. 2. an instrument for making a high note.
white	1. the colour of clean snow. 2. a part of an egg round the yolk.
whither	where: which place.
who	who is used in asking questions about persons. **Who** is that? We wondered **whose** voice we had heard.
whole	complete, with nothing missing. The drawing was **wholly** my own work.

why	for what reason. **Why** did you go?
wick	the tape which burns in candles and oil lamps.
wicked	evil: sinful.
wicket	1. the three stumps at cricket. 2. a small gate which is often part of a larger door.
wide	not narrow: broad. We had to guess the **width** of the road.
widow	a married woman whose husband is dead.
widower	a married man whose wife is dead.
wife	a married woman. The two **wives** went to the shops.
wig	false hair to cover the head.
wigwam	a Red Indian tent.
wild	1. fierce: not tame. 2. windy: stormy.
wilderness	a place where few plants grow: a lonely place.
wilful	1. done on purpose. 2. doing as we wish without thinking about other people.
will	1. a written paper saying who is to have our things when we are dead. 2. the power to choose what to do. The boy was always **willing** to help others.
willow	a tree with slender branches.
wilt	1. to wither. 2. to droop.
win	to beat the others: to be first. The boy was the **winner** of the race.
wince	to draw away because of pain: to flinch.
wind	(like 'pinned') quickly moving air. The day was fine but **windy.**
wind	(like 'mind') to turn and twist. The stream **wound** its way through the valley.
window	a frame in the wall of a building to allow light to enter. The worker came to repair the **window-pane.**
wine	the juice of crushed grapes made into a drink.
wing	1. the limb used by birds and insects for flying. 2. a part of an aeroplane.
wink	to blink with one eye.
winter	the coldest season of the year. In December we expect **wintry** weather.
wipe	to dry or clean with a cloth.
wire	metal made into lengths like string.

wireless	radio.
wisdom	being wise.
wise	sensible.
wish	to desire something very much.
wit	clever, amusing talk. We expected him to say something **witty**.
witch	a wicked woman who is supposed to have magic powers.
with	in the company of. The man was **with** his wife.
withdraw	to retire. He was injured, so he had to **withdraw** from the race.
within	inside. The goods were placed **within** the bag.
without	not having. We tried to leave **without** being seen.
wither	to fade away: to die slowly.
witness	a person who sees what happens.
wizard	a man with magic powers.
wobble	to stagger: to sway from one side to the other.
woe	sorrow: grief. The homeless people were a **woeful** sight.

wolf	a fierce wild animal like a wild dog. The **wolves** howled as they roamed through the forest.
woman	a grown female person. The two **women** had not met for several years.
wonder	1. surprise: amazement. The long procession was a **wonderful** sight. 2. to wish to know.
wood	1. a number of trees growing together. 2. timber. The goods came in a **wooden** box.
wool	the hair from the backs of sheep and lambs. The baby was playing with a **woolly** toy. The girl had knitted a **woollen** jumper.
word	1. a solemn promise. 2. letters together which make something we can understand and read.
work	something to do: labour. He was a **worker** on whom we could depend.
workshop	a place where work is done with tools.
world	the earth: the universe.
worm	a small crawling animal which lives in soil.
worn	when something has been used so much that it is of little further use.

worry	1. to feel anxious or troubled.
	2. to shake something in the teeth.
	The puppy **worried** the old slipper.
worse	not as good as.
	It was the **worst** snowstorm we had ever seen.
worship	to love and honour: to adore.
worth	value: importance.
	They were collecting for a **worthy** cause.
wound	an injury.
wrap	to cover something all round.
	The goods were placed in a paper **wrapper.**
wrath	great anger.
wreath	a circle or ring of leaves and flowers.
wreck	1. to spoil: to ruin.
	2. something which has been smashed to pieces.
wren	a small, brown bird with a sweet song.
wrestle	to struggle with a person and try to throw him to the ground.
wretch	a miserable and unhappy person.
	The shipwrecked sailors looked thoroughly **wretched.**
wriggle	to squirm: to twist about.
wring	to twist and squeeze something as tightly as possible.
wrinkle	a line or crease on the face or forehead.
wrist	the joint between the hand and the arm.
write	to set down words or letters so that they can be seen and read.
	We were unable to read the **writing.**
wrong	1. not right: incorrect.
	2. wicked.

X

X-rays	rays used to take photographs of things we cannot see.
xylophone	a musical instrument played by hitting bars with a wooden hammer.

Y

yacht	a racing or sailing boat.
yard	1. a measure of length.
	2. an enclosed space.
yarn	1. thread in long lengths.
	2. a tale: a story.
yawn	to open the mouth and breathe out when we are tired.
ye	you.
yea	yes.
year	twelve months: 52 weeks: 365 days: the time that the earth takes to go once round the sun.

yeast	a substance used in baking bread.
yell	to shout loudly.
yellow	a colour: the colour of the yolk of an egg. The leaves in autumn had a **yellowish** tint.
yesterday	the day before today.
yet	1. until now. 2. still.
yew	an evergreen tree with red berries.
yield	1. to give in. 2. to produce. The farmer hoped that the field would **yield** a good crop of wheat.
yoke	a harness for oxen.
yolk	the yellow centre part of an egg.
yonder	over there.

young	not old. John was **younger** than Jim, but Mary was the **youngest.**
your(s)	belonging to you. It seems as though you lost the ball **yourself.**
youth	a young man.
yule	Christmas.

Z

zeal	willingness: keenness to do good work.
zebra	an animal like a small horse but having a black and white, striped skin.
zero	nothing: '0'.
zigzag	moving sharply to one side and then to the other.
zone	a district: an area.
zoo	a place where wild animals are kept so that people may see them.

BOYS' CHRISTIAN NAMES

Adrian
Alan
Alastair
Albert
Alexander
Alfred
Andrew
Angus
Anthony
Arnold
Arthur
Aubrey
Austin

Barrie
Barry
Basil
Benjamin
Bertram
Brian
Bruce
Bryan

Cavan
Cecil
Cedric
Charles
Christopher
Clifford
Clive
Colin
Cyril

David
Denis

Dennis
Derek
Derick
Desmond
Donald
Douglas

Edgar
Edmund
Edward
Edwin
Eric
Ernest

Francis
Frank
Frederick

Garry
Geoffrey
George
Gerald
Gilbert
Glyn
Godfrey
Gordon
Graham

Harold
Harry
Henry
Herbert
Howard
Hugh

Iain
Ian
Ivor

Jack
James
Jeffrey
Jeremy
John
Jonathan
Joseph

Keith
Kenneth
Kevin

Laurence
Lawrence
Leonard
Leslie

Malcolm
Martin
Maurice
Melvin
Michael

Neil
Noel
Norman

Oliver
Owen

Patrick
Paul

Peter
Philip

Ralph
Raymond
Reginald
Richard
Robert
Rodney
Roger
Roland
Ronald
Roy
Rudolph

Sidney
Stanley
Stephen
Steven
Stewart
Stuart

Terence
Thomas
Timothy
Tom
Trevor
Tyrone

Victor
Vincent

Walter
Wilfred
William

GIRLS' CHRISTIAN NAMES

Alice
Alison
Amanda
Amy
Anabella
Andrea
Angela
Anita
Ann
Anna
Anne
Audrey
Avis
Avril

Barbara
Beatrice
Bernice
Beryl
Betty
Brenda
Bridget

Carol
Carole
Catherine
Cecily
Cicely
Cheryl
Christine
Clare
Constance
Corinne
Cynthia

Daisy
Daphne
Dawn
Deidre
Delia
Denise
Diane
Doreen
Doris
Dorothea
Dorothy

Edith
Edna
Eileen
Elaine
Eleanor
Elizabeth
Ellen
Elsie
Emily
Enid
Erica
Esther
Ethel
Eva
Evelyn

Florence
Frances
Freda

Georgina
Geraldine
Gladys
Glenda
Gloria
Glynis
Grace
Greta
Gwendoline

Hannah
Hazel
Heather
Helen
Hilary
Hilda

Ida
Irene
Iris
Isobel
Ivy

Jacqueline
Jane
Janet
Jayne
Jean
Jennifer

Jessica
Jessie
Jill
Joan
Joanna
Johanna
Josephine
Joy
Joyce
Judith
Julia
Julie
June

Karen
Kathleen
Kathryn
Kay

Laura
Lesley
Lilian
Linda
Lorna
Lorraine
Louise
Lucy
Lyn
Lynne

Madge
Margaret
Marguarita
Marjorie
Marie
Marilyn
Marion
Mary
Maureen
Mavis
Megan
Melanie
Mildred
Molly
Mona
Monica
Muriel

Nancy
Nina
Nora
Norah
Norma

Olive

Pamela
Patricia
Pauline
Peggy
Phyllis

Rena
Renee
Rhoda
Rita
Rosalind
Rose
Rosemary
Ruth

Sandra
Sara
Sarah
Sharon
Sheena
Sheila
Shirley
Stella
Susan
Sylvia

Teresa
Thora

Valerie
Vera
Veronica
Victoria
Violet

Wendy
Winifred

Yvonne

WORDS AND NUMBERS

one	first	twenty	twentieth
two	second	twenty-one	twenty-first
three	third	twenty-two	twenty-second
four	fourth	twenty-three	twenty-third
five	fifth	twenty-four	twenty-fourth
six	sixth	twenty-five	twenty-fifth
seven	seventh	twenty-six	twenty-sixth
eight	eighth	twenty-seven	twenty-seventh
nine	ninth	twenty-eight	twenty-eighth
ten	tenth	twenty-nine	twenty-ninth
eleven	eleventh	thirty	thirtieth
twelve	twelfth	forty	fortieth
thirteen	thirteenth	fifty	fiftieth
fourteen	fourteenth	sixty	sixtieth
fifteen	fifteenth	seventy	seventieth
sixteen	sixteenth	eighty	eightieth
seventeen	seventeenth	ninety	ninetieth
eighteen	eighteenth	hundred	hundredth
nineteen	nineteenth	thousand	thousandth

SCHOOL LESSONS

Activity
Arithmetic
Art

Basketry
Bookbinding

Cookery
Craft
Creative Writing

Dancing
Drama
Drawing

Elocution
Embroidery
English

French

Games
Geography

Handicraft
Handwork
History
Housecraft

Knitting

Language
Literature

Mathematics
Metalwork
Movement
Music

Nature Study
Needlework
Number

Orchestra

Painting
Physical Education
Physical Training
Poetry
Pottery
Projects

Reading
Religious Education
Religious Instruction

Science
Scripture
Sewing
Singing
Speech Training
Story

Topics

Woodwork
Writing

OBJECTS AND THEIR SOUNDS

an aeroplane **zooms**
an anvil **clangs**

a bell **clangs**
bells **peal**
bells **ring**
a bell **tinkles**

brakes **screech**

chains **clang**
a clock **chimes**
a clock **ticks**
coins **clink**
coins **jingle**
corks **pop**

dishes **rattle**
drums **beat**

an engine **chugs**
an engine **purrs**
an engine **throbs**

feet **patter**
feet **shuffle**
feet **tramp**

glass **tinkles**
a gun **booms**

a hinge **creaks**
hooves **clatter**

leaves **rustle**

paper **crinkles**

skirts **swish**
steam **hisses**

a telephone **rings**
a trumpet **blares**

water **laps**
a whip **cracks**
a whistle **shrieks**
the wind **sighs**
wood **crackles**

CREATURES AND THEIR SOUNDS

an ape **gibbers**
a bear **growls**
a bull **bellows**

a cat **purrs**
a cock **crows**
a cow **lows**

a dog **barks**
a donkey **brays**
a duck **quacks**

an elephant **trumpets**

a frog **croaks**

a hen **cackles**
a horse **neighs**

a lamb **bleats**
a lark **sings**

a monkey **chatters**
a mouse **squeaks**

an owl **hoots**

a pig **grunts**

a rabbit **squeals**
a robin **chirps**

a swallow **twitters**

a turkey **gobbles**

ABBREVIATIONS

A.A.	Automobile Association	h.p.	horse-power
A.D.	In the year of our Lord (Latin)	H.R.H.	Her (or His) Royal Highness
a.m.	before noon (Latin)	i.e.	that is (Latin)
B.B.C.	British Broadcasting Corporation	I.O.U.	I owe you
		J.P.	Justice of the Peace
B.C.	Before Christ	Ltd.	Limited
B.R.	British Rail	M.A.	Master of Arts
Co., Coy.	Company	M.P.	Member of Parliament
C.I.D.	Criminal Investigation Department	Mr.	Mister
		Mrs.	Mistress
C.O.D.	Cash on Delivery	O.H.M.S.	On Her (or His) Majesty's Service
do.	ditto (the same)	P.C.	Police Constable
Dr.	Doctor	P.O.	Post Office
e.g.	for example (Latin)	P.S.	written after (Latin)
E.R.	Elizabeth Regina (Queen Elizabeth)	P.T.O.	Please turn over
		R.A.C.	Royal Automobile Club
Esq.	Esquire	R.N.	Royal Navy
etc.	*et cetera* (Latin) and the other things	R.S.V.P.	Reply if you please (French)
		S.S.	Steam ship **or** Sailing ship
G.P.O.	General Post Office	U.K.	United Kingdom
H.M.	Her (or His) Majesty	U.S.A.	United States of America
H.M.S.	Her (or His) Majesty's Ship	U.S.S.R.	Union of Soviet Socialist Republics
		viz.	namely

WORDS ON THE CALENDAR

Sunday	January	July
Monday	February	August
Tuesday	March	September
Wednesday	April	October
Thursday	May	November
Friday	June	December
Saturday		

WORDS USED IN MATHEMATICS

abacus	digit	millimetre	quadrilateral
acute	divisor	minute	quotient
approximate		month	
arc	equilateral	multiple	radii
average	estimate		radius
axis			ratio
axes	fraction	negative	rectangle
		new halfpenny	reduction
		new penny	rightangle
binary	gramme	numerator	rotation
bisect	graph		
		obtuse	second
capacity	halfpenny	octagon	segment
centigrade	hexagon		series
centimetre	horizontal		square
centre	hour	parallel	symbol
circumference		parallelogram	
chord	isosceles	pendulum	tonne
compass		pentagon	triangle
compasses	kilogramme	penny	
cubic	kilometre	percentage	unit
		perimeter	unlike
day	litre	polygon	
decimal		positive	vertical
degree	mathematical	pound	
denominator	metre	prime	week
diagonal	metric	product	
diameter	millilitre	proportion	year

USEFUL BOOKS

We often wish to find out certain facts from books which we do not possess. It is useful to know the name of the book we need to tell us what we wish to know.

To find	*We need*
1. a telephone number	a telephone directory
2. the time of a train or bus	a time-table
3. the position of a certain place	an atlas
4. the facts about a certain place	a gazetteer
5. the meaning and correct spelling of a word	a dictionary
6. the day and date of the month	a calendar or diary
7. the cost of something for sale	a catalogue
8. attendance at school	an attendance register
9. a group of photographs	an album
10. a record of what has happened each day	a diary

CAPITAL LETTERS

Capital letters are used as follows:—

1. At the beginning of sentences.

John walked down the road. He was carrying a basket.

His sister, who was walking beside him, was wearing a brown coat. They were going to the shops to buy groceries.

2. For special names.

Names of people, roads, towns, cities, villages, countries, rivers, mountains, seas etc. are all written with capital letters.

Notice the capital letters in an address:—

Miss Joan Brown,
79, North Road,
GLASGOW, C.6.

J. Smith Esq.,
25, Bridge Street,
LONDON, E.7.

3. For names of God and Jesus Christ.

4. At the beginning of lines of poetry.

Away in a manger, no crib for a bed,
The little Lord Jesus lay down His sweet head,
The stars in the bright sky looked down where He lay,
The little Lord Jesus asleep on the hay.

5. When speech marks (inverted commas) are used for the first time.

Tom said: "We shall go to the cricket match tomorrow".

6. For the pronoun 'I' and for exclamation words such as 'Oh', 'Ah', etc.

7. For the important words in titles of books, stories, etc.

A Tale of Two Cities.
Jack and the Beanstalk.

Treasure Island.
Ali Baba and the Forty Thieves.

WORDS AND THEIR OPPOSITES

able	unable	clever	ignorant	fail	succeed
above	below	close	open	fair	dark
absent	present	coarse	fine	fall	rise
accept	decline	cold	hot	false	true
add	subtract	come	go	far	near
advance	retreat	content	discontent	farthest	nearest
after	before	correct	incorrect	fast	slow
agree	disagree	coward	hero	fat	thin
alive	dead			fertile	barren
always	never	danger	safety	fetch	take
ancient	modern	dark	light : fair	few	many
answer	question	day	night	fierce	gentle
arrive	depart	dead	alive	find	lose
asleep	awake	dear	cheap	finish	begin
attack	defend	decrease	increase	first	last
awake	asleep	deep	shallow	fit	unfit
		defeat	victory	float	sink
back	front	depart	arrive	flow	ebb
backward	forward	depth	height	foe	friend
bad	good	descend	ascend	foolish	wise
beautiful	ugly	die	live	forget	remember
before	after	difficult	easy	found	lost
begin	cease	dirty	clean	freedom	captivity
behind	before	divide	multiply	freeze	thaw
believe	disbelieve	down	up	friend	foe
below	above	dry	wet	from	to
bent	straight	dull	shiny	front	back
better	worse	dwarf	giant	full	empty
big	little			further	nearer
bitter	sweet	early	late	future	past
black	white	east	west		
borrow	lend	easy	difficult	gain	loss
bottom	top	ebb	flow	gay	miserable
bravery	cowardice	either	neither	generous	mean
break	mend	empty	full	gentle	fierce
bright	dull	end	beginning	give	take
broad	narrow	enemy	friend	glad	sorry
build	destroy	entrance	exit	go	come
buy	sell	even	odd	good	bad
		evening	morning	great	small
calm	rough	ever	never	grief	happiness
cease	begin	everywhere	nowhere	guilty	innocent
cellar	attic	exit	entrance		
cheap	dear	expand	contract	happy	unhappy : sad
clean	dirty	export	import	hard	soft
clear	cloudy			hate	love

WORDS AND THEIR OPPOSITES—*continued*

head	tail: foot	lost	found	plenty	few
heat	cold	loud	soft	plural	singular
heavy	light	love	hate	polite	impolite
height	depth	low	high	poor	rich
here	there			popular	unpopular
hide	seek	many	few	possess	dispossess
high	low	mean	generous	possible	impossible
hit	miss	meek	proud	praise	blame
honest	dishonest	merry	sad	presence	absence
hot	cold	mild	keen: bitter	present	absent
huge	tiny	misery	happiness	pretty	ugly
humble	haughty	miss	nit	private	public
		modern	ancient	proper	improper
idle	hardworking	more	less	proud	humble
ignorant	clever	morning	evening	pure	impure
ill	well	mountain	valley	put	take
immense	tiny	mourn	rejoice		
import	export	multiply	divide	question	answer
increase	decrease			quick	slow
innocent	guilty	near	far	quiet	noisy
inside	outside	neither	either		
		never	always	raise	lower
join	separate	new	old	rapid	slow
joy	sorrow	night	day	rare	common
junior	senior	no	yes	ready	unready
		noble	ignoble	reap	sow
kind	unkind	none	some	rear	front: van
		north	south	receive	give
land	sea	nothing	something	refuse	accept
large	small	now	then	regular	irregular
last	first	nowhere	everywhere	reliable	unreliable
late	early			remember	forget
lazy	industrious	odd	even	retreat	advance
lead	follow	off	on	rich	poor
lean	fat	often	seldom	right	wrong
least	most	old	young	rise	fall
leave	arrive	open	shut	rough	smooth
left	right	out	in	rude	polite
less	more	over	under		
liberty	captivity			sad	happy
light	heavy: dark	past	future	safety	danger
like	unlike	peace	war	scarce	plentiful
little	big	permanent	temporary	seldom	often
live	die	plain	fancy	selfish	generous
lock	unlock	pleasant	unpleasant	sell	buy
long	short	please	displease	send	receive
lose	gain			senior	junior

WORDS AND THEIR OPPOSITES—*continued*

sense	nonsense	tall	short	vacant	full
shallow	deep	tame	wild	valley	mountain
short	long	teach	learn	victory	defeat
sink	swim	thaw	freeze	visible	invisible
slow	fast	there	here		
small	large	thick	thin	war	peace
smooth	rough	this	that	warm	cold
soft	hard	tidy	untidy	wax	wane
solid	liquid	tight	slack	weak	strong
sour	sweet	timid	bold	wealth	poverty
south	north	tiny	huge	well	unwell: ill
sow	reap	to	fro	west	east
spend	save	top	bottom	wet	dry
stale	fresh	true	false	white	black
stern	bow	trust	distrust	wide	narrow
still	moving	truth	untruth	wild	tame
stop	go			win	lose
straight	bent			wind	unwind
strong	weak	ugly	pretty	winter	summer
subtract	add	under	over	wise	unwise
succeed	fail	undo	fasten	with	without
summer	winter	up	down	wrap	unwrap
sweet	sour	upper	lower	wrong	right
swim	sink	upward	downward		
		useful	useless	yes	no
tail	head	usual	unusual	young	old
take	give				